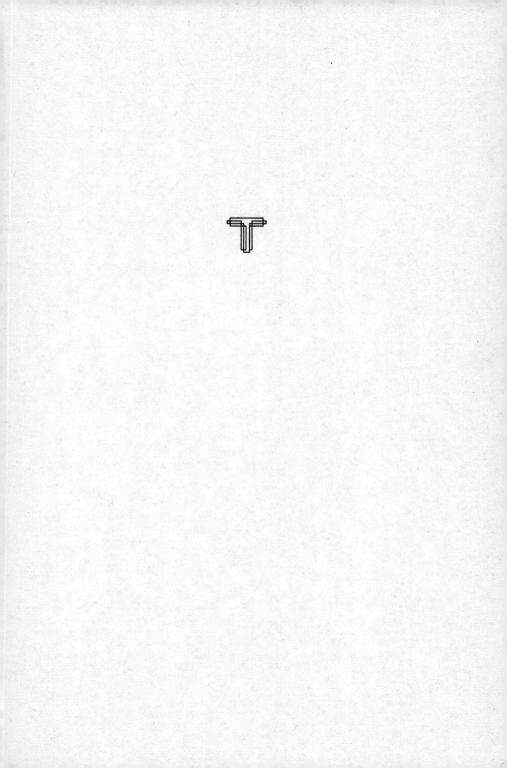

AS YOU WISH

INCONCEIVABLE TALES FROM
THE MAKING OF

✢ THE ✢

PRINCESS BRIDE

CARY ELWES

WITH JOE LAYDEN

A TOUCHSTONE BOOK

NEW YORK   LONDON   TORONTO   SYDNEY   NEW DELHI

Touchstone
An Imprint of Simon & Schuster, Inc.
1230 Avenue of the Americas
New York, NY 10020

First Touchstone paperback edition October 2016

TOUCHSTONE and colophon are
registered trademarks of Simon & Schuster, Inc.

Unless otherwise credited, all photographs are courtesy of *The Princess Bride*, Ltd.

For information about special discounts for bulk purchases,
please contact Simon & Schuster Special Sales at
1-866-506-1949 or business@simonandschuster.com.

The Simon & Schuster Speakers Bureau can bring authors to your live event.
For more information or to book an event contact the Simon & Schuster Speakers
Bureau at 1-866-248-3049 or visit our website at www.simonspeakers.com.

Interior design by Ruth Lee-Mui

Manufactured in the United States of America

10   9   8

The Library of Congress has cataloged the hardcover edition as follows:
Elwes, Cary.
   As you wish : inconceivable tales from the making of The princess bride / Cary Elwes
with Joe Layden.
      pages   cm
   Includes index.
   1. Princess bride (Motion picture)   2. Elwes, Cary.   I. Layden, Joe.   II. Title.
PN1997.P74534E69 2014
   791.43'72—dc23   2014014652

ISBN 978-1-4767-6402-3
ISBN 978-1-4767-6404-7 (pbk)
ISBN 978-1-4767-6403-0 (ebook)

For my little princess, Dominique

CONTENTS

Contents

AS YOU WISH

FOREWORD

William Goldman once said about the movie business, "Nobody knows anything." *The Princess Bride* is Exhibit A in defense of that truism.

As I was starting my career as a filmmaker, I thought, naively, Why not make a film based on *The Princess Bride?* That should be easy. It's a brilliant story written by one of America's greatest writers. Why wouldn't everyone just jump at this idea? Little did I know that for fifteen years it had been the story that no studio would touch. Fortunately, Norman Lear, my *All in the Family* boss, and the man whom I would come to call my second father, had faith in this wonderful fractured fairy tale.

Making *The Princess Bride* was one of the greatest experiences of my life. Living in England for six months, working with old friends, and people who would become old friends, creating a film based on my favorite book of all time. Nothing could be more satisfying.

When you start a film, you have an idea of what you want it to become, but you never know if anyone else will share your interest. Bill Goldman once referred to the book he wanted on his tombstone as an oddball story. When it came time for the movie's release, no one had any idea of how to sell it. Was it a fairy tale? Was it a swashbuckling adventure? Was it a love story? Or was it just a nutty satire? The fact is it was, and is, all of the above. Not easy to capture in a two-minute preview trailer or a thirty-second TV ad.

We opened to some critical success, but only moderate business. Luckily through VHS, DVD, and TV it managed to take hold, and over the past twenty-five years its popularity has grown. I can't tell you the pleasure I get from people who first saw it when they were kids, telling me how much their kids love it. What a thrill to know that a film you've had a hand in is getting passed down to future generations.

Reading Cary's book has brought back wonderful memories. He has so beautifully recounted what was for me, and I'm sure for all of us, one of the truly great creative experiences of our lives. He takes us, as only he can, through the Man in Black's eye view of the world of the R.O.U.S., Miracle Max, and the Cliffs of Insanity. And he does it with style and grace. So curl up in a comfy spot and have fun storming the castle.

—*Rob Reiner*

INTRODUCTION

S tanding onstage at Alice Tully Hall at Lincoln Center, surrounded by cast members and some of the crew, many of whom I've not seen in years, I feel an almost overwhelming sense of gratitude and nostalgia. We have gathered here at the New York Film Festival to celebrate the twenty-fifth anniversary of *The Princess Bride*, a movie whose popularity and resonance now span generations.

That fact alone boggles the mind—how such a quirky and modestly conceived film could achieve such a lofty position in the pantheon of popular culture. What really strikes me, though, as I look down the row at the faces of my fellow actors, is how quickly the time has passed. Has it really been twenty-five years? A quarter century? The passing of time is most critically noted by those who are missing, the great Peter Falk and that gentle mountain of a man, André the Giant. But to counter that sadness is the camaraderie of being back with those who are here tonight and who stood alongside me so many years ago: Rob Reiner, Billy Crystal, Carol Kane, Wallace Shawn, Chris Sarandon, and Mandy Patinkin, not to mention Robin Wright, looking as lovely as she did the day I first laid eyes on her so many years ago. Then again, she has always set a rather ridiculously high standard for beauty, and that seems not to have changed. The only ones who couldn't make it were Christopher Guest and Fred Savage, who unfortunately were busy working on other projects.

This is a night of red carpets and remembrance, of interviews and a screening filled with laughter and joy. It is also only the third time that I have seen the film in its entirety with an audience since its initial screening in 1987 at the Toronto Film Festival. That previous event, while successful, did not exactly produce the sort of response one would expect of a film destined to become a classic.

Is it fair to call *The Princess Bride* a classic? The storybook story about pirates and princesses, giants and wizards, Cliffs of Insanity and Rodents of Unusual Size? It's certainly one of the most often quoted films in cinema history, with lines like:

* *"Hello. My name is Inigo Montoya. You killed my father. Prepare to die."*
* *"Inconceivable!"*
* *"Anybody want a peanut?"*
* *"Have fun storming the castle."*
* *"Never get involved in a land war in Asia."*
* *"Life is pain, Highness. Anyone who says differently is selling something."*
* *"Rest well, and dream of large women."*
* *"I hate for people to die embarrassed."*
* *"Please consider me as an alternative to suicide."*
* *"This is true love. You think this happens every day?"*
* *"Get used to disappointment."*

* "I'm not a witch. I'm your wife."
* "Mawidge. That bwessed awangement!"
* "You seem a decent fellow. I hate to kill you" . . . "You seem a decent fellow. I hate to die."
* "Death cannot stop true love. All it can do is delay it for a while."
* "Never go in against a Sicilian when death is on the line!"
* "There's a shortage of perfect breasts in this world. It would be a pity to damage yours."

And of course . . .

"As you wish."

Classic: a small word that carries enormous weight, although sometimes it's tossed around a bit too casually; a reputation earned over the course of time, and given only to those rare films that stand up to repeated viewings. That being said, *The Princess Bride* has aged remarkably well. I think this is in part because of the quality of the writing, the directing, and the wonderful ensemble of actors I had the sheer pleasure of working with.

Even though it is the fans who have truly kept the memory of the movie alive, each of us in the cast has remembrances of making the film, things that have stayed with us over the years. All of us have stories about encounters or moments, like being approached and asked to recite a favorite *Princess Bride* line. Mandy swears that barely a day goes by that he isn't asked by someone, somewhere, to recite Inigo Montoya's most famous words, in which he vows vengeance on behalf of his father.

"And I never let them down," he says.

I read somewhere recently that a passenger on a plane was asked to leave the flight as his Montoya T-shirt bearing that infamous line frightened one of the passengers who had never seen the movie. After it was explained to them, apparently the T-shirted passenger was allowed to stay on the aircraft.

Mandy, himself, has a long and impressive résumé. The man has won a Tony, an Emmy, and countless other honors. But, like most of us at Lincoln Center tonight, he knows that someday his obituary will feature, more prominently than anything else, his affiliation with *The Princess Bride*.

And that's just fine with him, as it is with all of us.

There might be a shortage of perfect breasts in the world, but there is no shortage of actors who achieve a degree of recognition or fame due to the popularity (or, in some cases, the ignominy, which is an entirely different story) of a specific movie and their role within that movie. It can become a blessing or a curse; sometimes a little of both, depending on the circumstances. Over the past three decades I've appeared in nearly a hundred movies and television shows. I've been a leading man and a supporting actor and worked in almost every genre. But whatever else I've done or whatever else I might do, *The Princess Bride* will always be the work with which I am most closely associated; and Westley, with his wisp of a mustache and ponytail, the character with whom I will be forever linked.

Not *Glory*, which earned higher critical praise upon release and won more awards; not *Days of Thunder* or *Twister*, both of which were summer blockbusters. Not even *Saw*, which was shot in eighteen days on a budget smaller than most movies spend on catering, and earned more than $100 million; and that's just fine by me.

When I started *The Princess Bride* I was very young and fairly new to the world of film. I was cast in a movie that frankly could have been interpreted as preposterous, were it not for the fact that it was so well written, so well directed, and populated with such a ridiculously talented cast. As I look around the stage at Rob Reiner, the director, and William Goldman, the writer, who so deftly and lovingly adapted the screenplay from his equally imaginative novel, I think how incredibly fortunate I was to have been part of this project. To have been plucked from relative obscurity and dropped onto a set with these two insanely talented men and this extraordinary cast.

I'd be lying if I told you we had even the slightest inkling that our movie, made on a modest budget over a period of less than four months, and shot in and around London and the magnificent Peak District of Derbyshire, was destined to become a classic. But I think it withstands the rigors of time because it seems to be a timeless story—a tale of love and romance. Of heroes and villains. And, although it is a film from the 1980s, there is nothing on the screen that betrays its birth date (notwithstanding perhaps the Rodents of Unusual Size).

Instead of a bouncy techno-pop sound track, you have the elegant slide guitar of Mark Knopfler; instead of big hair and shoulder pads, you have the period style of a swashbuckler and a princess. Perhaps the only thing that serves as a time stamp is Fred Savage's video game at the very start of the movie (which, by the way, is where the film gets its first laugh). It is, of course, a movie within a movie. A story within a story, much like the book itself. Even in the scenes between Peter Falk and Fred Savage, a grandfather reading to his bedridden sick grandson, there is a timeless grace and elegance to the filmmaking. And then there is the dialogue:

"They're kissing again. Do we have to read the kissing parts?"

What preteen boy hasn't said that or thought that? Or at least something like that? It's the kind of dialogue that holds up. It endures. In fact, like a good wine without iocane powder, it seems to get better with time.

The movie, believe it or not, opened to mostly positive, if occasionally befuddled, critical response. Even those who praised the movie weren't quite sure what to think. Was it a comedy? A romance? An adventure story? A fantasy? The fact is, it was all of those things and more. But Hollywood abhors that which is not easily categorized, and so the film didn't quite gain the kind of traction it might have deserved, grossing a respectable, though hardly overwhelming, $30.8 million in its first run ($60 million when adjusted for inflation). This meant it made almost twice the budget, but still only a tenth of what that year's top-grossing movie, *Fatal Attraction,* made only the week before.

Within a few months of finishing the movie, we all moved on with our lives, putting *The Princess Bride* in our respective rearview mirrors. There were other projects, other films, families to raise, careers to nurture. And then—though I can't pinpoint the time when it actually occurred—a strange thing began to happen: *The Princess Bride* came back to life. Much of this can be attributed to timing—in particular to the newly developing video market. *The Princess Bride* came to be enormously popular in the VHS format. And it was via this relatively new medium that the film began to gain traction, and not simply as a rental. After careful scrutiny by those who do these things, it became clear that fans were not only recommending it to friends and family members, they also began purchasing a copy for their own home libraries. It became that rare kind of movie that was viewed and enjoyed, and ultimately beloved by entire families. Copies of it were being passed down from generation to generation in much the same manner that children were introduced to the magic of *The Wizard of Oz* by nostalgic parents who wanted to share one of their favorite movies. So, too, was *The Princess Bride* uniquely family entertainment. Parents with their children, and even their grandchildren, could watch the movie together, and each enjoy it for what it was. There was nothing condescending or embarrassing about it. Nothing offensive. It seemed to be as smart and funny on the tenth viewing as it was on the first.

Today *The Princess Bride* is acknowledged and recognized as one of the more popular and successful films in Hollywood history. It is ranked among the 100 Greatest Film Love Stories by the American Film Institute, is on Bravo's list of the 100 Funniest Movies, and Goldman's script is ranked by the Writers Guild of America as one of the top 100 screenplays ever produced.

All of these things, and a whole lot more, were running through my head that night at Lincoln Center. At some point during the evening, we all were asked what the movie meant to us. There wasn't time for me to adequately put into words exactly how I felt, so that's what I'm trying to do now with this book. The film really gave me a career in the arts and the life that I have today, a life I feel privileged to enjoy. That's not an overstatement. Other movies have surely helped, but this was the one that put me on the map and allowed me to stay there.

I still get fan mail today from children all over the world, sending me drawings and sketches of pirates dueling, or of princesses kissing them. I even have to be careful not to walk down the wrong aisle at Toys "R" Us, lest I find myself suddenly under siege by little tykes with plastic swords and shields.

Everyone associated with the film has heard stories by now of *Princess Bride* weddings, where the bride and groom are dressed as Buttercup and Westley and the pastor even recites Peter Cook's dialogue from the movie. Or the late-night dress-up interactive screenings, not unlike the ones they do for *The Rocky Horror Picture Show*, where things like peanuts are thrown at the screen after Fezzik's now famous line. The *Princess Bride* nights at the Alamo Drafthouse cinemas, a national restaurant/movie house, have become so popular that they now produce their own licensed *Princess Bride* wine.

I can't speak for everyone, but I consider it a blessing. Clearly *The Princess Bride* has become a truly remarkable phenomenon. The film has literally millions of devotees. They know every line, every character, every scene. And, if they'd like to know a little bit more about how their favorite film was made, as seen through the eyes of a young actor who got much more than he bargained for, then all I can say is . . . *As you wish.*

MEETING ROB

BERLIN, JUNE 29, 1986

The note simply read: IMPORTANT.

It was a message from my agent, Harriet Robinson, that had been slipped under my door by a bellhop at the Hotel Kempinski, where I was staying.

I immediately picked up the phone and dialed her number. This would be the call that actually changed my life. After I reached Harriet on the line she began to tell me that she had arranged an important meeting for me. That the director of *This Is Spinal Tap*, Rob Reiner, and his producing partner, Andy Scheinman, were planning on coming to Berlin to see me.

"Really?"

"Yes."

"What for?"

She said they were hamstrung by a tight preproduction schedule and were still looking for an actor to play the pivotal role of Westley in a film version of *The Princess Bride.*

"Not *The Princess Bride* by William Goldman?"

"I think so, yes," came the response.

I couldn't believe it. This was a book I had read when I was just thirteen. And here I was being considered for one of the leads by the director and the producer. Fortunately, for me, they did not change their plans.

A little backstory on where I was at that time. I was a neophyte, just twenty-three, with only a handful of films to my credit. But I already knew what I wanted out of life. I knew I wanted to be an actor. I was born and raised in London and briefly attended the London Academy of Music & Dramatic Art, one of the world's most prestigious training grounds for serious stage actors. I enjoyed studying but my ultimate goal back then was simply to be a working actor, preferably in film. Besides, I had already done plenty of studying when I moved to New York to attend the Actors Studio and the Lee Strasberg Theatre & Film Institute. After leaving LAMDA, I picked up an agent, Harriet, and started going out on auditions.

I'd already been a production assistant on a handful of movies, including the James Bond feature *Octopussy*, where I had the unique experience of being asked to drive Bond himself, Roger Moore, to work a couple of times. I was a nervous wreck, I can tell you. All that kept going through my mind was, What if I killed Bond on the way to work in a traffic accident? How'd that be? It would certainly put a halt to my burgeoning career in the film industry. I could already see the headlines: "Lowly Production Assistant Kills Bond!" During one of our early-morning drives, Mr. Moore actually looked up from his newspaper and said, in that very calm and collected manner of his, "You can speed up a little if you want to."

By the mid-1980s, I had a résumé that was short but not unimpressive. My first movie, released in 1984, was *Another Country*, a historical drama based on a popular West End play by Julian Mitchell, with Rupert Everett and Colin Firth. I had costarred with Helena Bonham Carter in *Lady Jane*, director Trevor Nunn's period drama about Lady Jane Grey, the nine-day queen of England whose brief reign followed the death of King Edward VI. Apparently this was the film that Rob had been able to see, and the one that convinced him to take a chance on me.

After I wrapped *Lady Jane*, Trevor Nunn offered me an opportunity to spend a year in residency with the Royal Shakespeare Company, of which he was the director. I was flattered almost to the point of distraction—most young actors would kill for such an opportunity. But by this time I was living in London, and I knew that spending a year with the RSC, as prestigious as it was, would be the equivalent of doing graduate work in theater: the compensation wouldn't even cover my rent. Nevertheless, I seriously considered the offer, as it came from a talented director whom I admired and still admire a great deal. Might things have been different for me had I said yes? Who knows? I have very few regrets about the life I've been fortunate to lead. But this much seems certain: if I had taken up residency with the RSC, I would not have been free to accept the role of Westley. In fact, I might not have even been considered. You could say I was rather lucky, for as it turned out, I happened to be in the right place at the right time.

By the time Rob Reiner had started looking for someone to play his leading man, I had a body of work that was thin but perhaps worth investigating. Through fate or skilled representation or a combination of these I came under consideration for the role of the farmhand turned pirate, Westley—a character created in a renowned novel that had long been considered incapable of being adapted for the screen. And one that I had already read and enjoyed as a kid.

How did that come to be? Well, it turns out my stepfather had worked in the literary department of the William Morris Agency in Los Angeles and, after leaving to make movies, had produced William Goldman's very first screenplay, adapted from the novel *The Moving Target*, by Ross Macdonald. The film version was released in 1966 under that same title in Britain but was renamed *Harper* for release in the United States, where it became a modest hit and helped further establish the stardom of its young lead, Paul Newman. And it wasn't bad for Goldman, either, who won an Edgar Award for best screenplay and subsequently became one of the hottest writers in Hollywood.

Being a huge fan of Goldman's, my stepfather naturally kept a copy of *The Princess Bride* in his library and one day gave it to me to read. Needless to say, I loved it. I remember reading the author's own description of the "good bits" from S. Morgenstern's fictitious novel:

Fencing. Fighting. Torture. Poison. True love. Hate. Revenge. Giants. Hunters. Bad men. Good men. Beautiful ladies. Snakes. Spiders. Pain. Death. Brave men. Cowardly men. Strongest men. Chases. Escapes. Lies. Truths. Passion. Miracles.

Now if that didn't sound exciting to a thirteen-year-old, nothing would.

When the call came from Harriet, I was in Berlin shooting a little indie film called *Maschenka*, based on a semiautobiographical novel by Vladimir Nabokov, the man who gave us one of the most controversial examples of twentieth-century literature, *Lolita*. The film was a British-Finnish-German coproduction and was being shot in both Germany and Finland.

This was the early summer of 1986, only a few months after the Chernobyl nuclear disaster, which had caused quite a fear at the time. Harriet actually told me that Rob and Andy had seriously thought about canceling their trip because of "the whole nuclear thing." My recollection is that it wasn't of much concern to those of us working on our small European coproduction. I recall a crew meeting being called on a set in a place called Katajanokka, in Helsinki, only a week before and being told that there was nothing to fear because the winds were in our favor and that the fallout was likely to be blown in another direction. We *were* warned, however, that as a precaution we probably shouldn't drink the local milk. At least not until it had been declared safe. Like a good many of the others on the crew, I went back to work, scratching my head, wondering if we shouldn't be taking the whole thing more seriously. We were, after all, only eight hundred miles away from the accident. All I can say is that insurance policies for the film industry back then were not as sophisticated as they are now, so shutting down production wasn't really an option.

Anyway, not exactly what you want to hear, but the show did indeed go on. And, as far as I know, no one got sick from the experience, thank God. The last few weeks of the shoot took place in Berlin at Studio Babelsberg, which is how I came to be staying at the Kempinski.

I pressed for more information from Harriet. She said all she knew was that Rob and Andy were trying to meet as many British actors who might be right for the part, and that they were obviously interested in me. I subsequently found out that Rob had gotten a call from the casting director, Jane Jenkins, suggesting that he watch *Lady Jane*, and if he liked it, fly out to meet me. It seemed reasonable to think that I was in good shape if they were traveling such a long way—and not only that but to a region that might be contaminated with radioactive material. I wasn't accustomed to this level of interest, and (even though it happens quite often now) no director had ever come to visit me on location before.

"Do I have to read for the part?" I asked, dreading the answer.

"It's possible, since they're coming all that way," Harriet replied.

As an actor you lose far more roles than you gain at readings. You learn pretty early on that most things are beyond your control, and that it is better to "let go and let God" and to "get used to disappointment," as Goldman so eloquently had the Man in Black say in the movie. I kept trying to tell myself there would always be another film, another job on the horizon—that it didn't matter. But deep down I knew I wasn't kidding anyone, least of all myself. This was far from being "just another job." This was two of my heroes, Bill Goldman and Rob Reiner, working together!

Although the novel was published in 1973 to immediate acclaim and passionate reader response, it was already thirteen years old by the time I was approached to play the role of Westley. Goldman's screenplay, which he had adapted from his own book, had in fact become something of a legendary property in Hollywood circles, having been declared by those in power at the studios as an impossible film to make.

Having arduously penned the script himself, Goldman had long declared it to be his favorite among those he had written. High praise, given that by this time his oeuvre included *Marathon Man, Butch Cassidy and the Sundance Kid,* and *All the President's Men,* the last two earning him Academy Awards for screenwriting.

ANDY SCHEINMAN
We were trying to meet all the actors who might be capable of playing Westley, and I seem to remember Colin Firth was one of them. We get a call saying there's this kid you should see, he's in East Germany. So all I remember is it was right after Chernobyl. And I'm not crazy about going to East Germany. I'm looking at maps, and they have gray areas where the nuclear fallout is and I don't like it. And Rob was like, "Don't go if you don't want to." But I did. I just remember running fast into the hotel, like that's going to do anything. And literally leaving a thousand-dollar jacket behind. I didn't have that much money and I certainly didn't have any other jackets like that, but I couldn't wear it anymore. I just left it.

And yet, despite Goldman's impressive résumé and passion for the piece, the project seemed destined to languish in what is commonly known in the business as "Development Hell"—meaning it had been passed around the studios a lot with all of them either unable to get it made, or simply uninterested. As Goldman himself once famously put it, "Even François Truffaut couldn't make this movie."

WILLIAM GOLDMAN
I was going to California on a trip, and I told my daughters, "I'll write you a story; what do you want it to be about?" And one of them said, "Princesses!" and the other said something about "brides." And I said, "Okay, that will be the title." I went out and wrote the first two pages and then I stopped. And then years later I went back and finished the book.

It became this legendary unproduced script, even being mentioned in the prestigious French film journal *Cahiers du Cinéma* as such. And so it seemed that the author's favorite work was destined never to see the light of day . . . that is, until it fell into the right hands.

For those of you unaware, it should be noted that Rob Reiner's career was on a clear upward trajectory by this point. No longer merely a sitcom star, he'd proven himself to be an A-list director with a deft ability to meld genres with his work on *The Sure Thing* and especially *This Is Spinal Tap*, released in 1984. Everyone who cared about rock music or comedy instantly fell in love with the movie and memorized its largely improvised dialogue. It was the first and maybe the best of what would become a new category of film and television: the mock documentary (or "mockumentary"), and it was Rob who steered the project expertly from its conception to the cult status it now enjoys, even among musicians. Tom Petty once declared his fondness for the dim-witted, aging rock stars by revealing that he and his bandmates routinely gather and recite lines from the film before going onstage. Rob also told me that when he met with Sting about playing Humperdinck, the musician told him he had watched *Spinal Tap* over fifty times and that every time he "didn't know whether to laugh or cry." For a director or writer (Rob's coauthors on that film were Harry Shearer, Michael McKean, and Christopher Guest, who would be among the *Princess Bride* ensemble), that has to be just about the highest praise imaginable.

Around this same time Rob was putting the finishing touches on *Stand by Me*, an adaptation of a Stephen King novella that would be recognized as one of the best coming-of-age stories Hollywood has ever produced. Later on, after I arrived in London, he arranged a private screening for me at Pinewood Studios, and I remember being deeply moved by it. I hadn't seen that kind of honest acting from kids since watching Truffaut's *The 400 Blows*. It was clear to me that from *This Is Spinal Tap* to *The Sure Thing* to *Stand by Me*, Rob was basically on a winning streak. His films were all very different in tone and genre, and they all ended up doing very good business. He was a director with a unique vision who made memorable films. There was really no one else doing the kind of work that he was doing. So with that impressive body of work behind him, Rob had earned the right to choose his next project based primarily on what he wanted to do rather than what was expected of him. Essentially, he was given carte blanche. As I understand it, the conversation between Rob and the then head of Columbia Pictures, which was releasing *Stand by Me*, went something like this:

"Anything you want," the studio head told him. "Anything at all."

"Really? Anything?" Rob responded with glee.

"Yes."

"In that case I want to do my favorite book," Rob replied.

"What's that?"

"The Princess Bride."

"Anything but that!" came the instantaneous response.

And so for a while the project seemed to stall.

But, to Rob's credit, he was steadfast. Although he has an extraordinarily warm and generous spirit, and is not at all prone to the sort of rampant ego that is not uncommon among some of the upper echelon of Hollywood talent, he is hardly a pushover. In fact, it was his sheer determination and his vision that were largely responsible for making the film happen.

Time has obviously proven that Rob was the right man for the job. Like most people who read it, he had been a huge fan of the novel. He also had supreme confidence in his ability to blend all the different genres that filled its pages: romance, adventure, fantasy, drama, comedy, action. He would take these elements and turn them on their heads. He would have fun doing it and, in turn, create a movie that would be fun for others. To accomplish that task requires a very sure hand, and I don't believe many filmmakers then or now could have pulled it off.

With apologies to Bill Goldman, who dislikes the term, Rob really was, for lack of a better description, a

ANDY SCHEINMAN

By this time, Rob's dad, Carl Reiner, had already been approached by Bill Goldman about doing the project. But Carl either didn't have time or couldn't figure out how to do it, or whatever. For whatever reason, it just didn't happen. It was about thirteen years later that Rob said to me, "I think it's a great book and I think we should see if we can pull it off."

At one point we had almost had it set up at Columbia Pictures. That's when I heard one of my favorite lines in the movie business. The head of Columbia said, "You've got to be careful with William Goldman scripts. He tricks you with good writing."

ROB REINER

I had been a huge fan of Goldman's from the first book he ever wrote, which was *The Temple of Gold*, and then *Your Turn to Curtsy, My Turn to Bow*. I read literally every book he had ever written. He was doing a book about one season on Broadway in 1968 called *The Season*, and my dad had had a play on that year, titled *Something Different*, which Bill had devoted a chapter of his book to. Shortly thereafter, Bill finished *The Princess Bride* and sent it to my father to see if he was interested in making it into a movie. But he really didn't know what to do with it. I don't even know if he ever read it or not, but he gave it to me because he knew I was such a big fan of Goldman's. I was in my twenties at the time and I hadn't directed anything. I read it and it was just one of those experiences when you're reading something, you think the writer is in your head. Everything in the book was like, Oh, my God, I'm so in sync with this sensibility here. I mean, I just fell in love with it. It was like the best thing I'd ever read. And so time goes by and I'd done *All in the Family* and then I started my directing career. And after the first couple of movies I started thinking, Well, they make movies out of books, and I started thinking about what book did I really enjoy, and I remembered *The Princess Bride* was my favorite book of all time. So I naively said, "I wonder if we could make a movie out of that." I had no idea at the time that a lot of people had already tried: Norman Jewison, Robert Redford, François Truffaut. It was in one of those cinema books as one of the greatest screenplays ever written that had never been produced. I had my agency get in touch with Bill to see if he would be willing to meet with me. He had seen *Spinal Tap*, and I was just finishing up my second movie, *The Sure Thing*. It was still in a rough-cut form, but I arranged a screening for him to see it. This was all just for Bill to agree to meet with me.

young auteur. One whose success had left him with nearly complete artistic control over his projects. He was able to release his films the way he wanted them to look, as he had final cut in the editing rooms, something that hardly exists today. And he used his clout not to accumulate staggering wealth with superficial blockbusters, but rather to tackle something far more ambitious. Something near and dear to his heart.

How could one not admire that?

Apparently the same studio head at Columbia ended up telling Rob, "You'll never get the rights anyway, as Goldman will never let anyone make it!"

So Rob decided to go ahead and try to meet with Goldman, who by that time had reacquired the rights to his own novel, to see if he could convince Goldman to let him have the material. He took with him the person who accompanied him to all his meetings: his producing partner, Andy Scheinman. It turned out the studio head had indeed been accurate in describing Goldman's reticence to let the movie be made. As Rob and Andy were to soon discover, the writer had evidently nearly lost all enthusiasm for the movie business. He hadn't liked the way the studios had dealt with him in the past, especially when it came to this, his favorite project. Nor had he had any luck with them, or with anyone else for that matter, trying to get it made.

In order to better understand Mr. Goldman's frame of mind I should perhaps furnish you with a little history about the various attempts to make the picture. As I understand it, at one point the project was initially a "go" at 20th Century Fox, which had purchased the book before it was even published, with Richard Lester (famous for the Beatles movies *A Hard Day's Night* and *Help!*) attached to direct. That was when who Goldman refers to as the "Greenlight Guy" (i.e., the person who decides which projects are to be made for the studio) was fired at Fox. Then, as luck would have it, the next Greenlight Guy proceeded to clear his desk of all his predecessor's work (a surprisingly not uncommon occurrence in our business) so that he could start with a clean slate. Which is when Goldman bought the rights to his book back from Fox (unheard of to this day, I imagine), to protect his cherished work and prevent them from letting someone else rewrite the script. As Bill wrote in the twenty-fifth-anniversary edition of the book, he felt he was "the only idiot who could destroy it now."

By this time no other major studio was willing to touch the material but one. And believe it or not, the Greenlight Guy was in the middle of negotiating with Goldman when he, too, was fired over the weekend just as the deal was about to close. Another small movie studio literally folded during negotiations. At one point Norman Jewison, famous for having directed *Jesus Christ Superstar, Fiddler on the Roof,* and *Moonstruck,* was going to make it as an independent film but he couldn't raise the money even with a then virtually unknown Arnold Schwarzenegger attached to play the role of Fezzik. After that, John Boorman, Robert Redford, and even François Truffaut tried their hand at getting the movie made but somehow couldn't get it off the ground.

And so it made sense that Goldman was naturally reticent to let his heart get excited all over again only to be potentially disappointed. I guess he hadn't gotten "used to disappointment" when it came to this particular project.

Fortunately for Rob and for us all, he finally got Goldman's blessing, which was a feat in itself. He then went to his mentor, producer Norman Lear (the genius behind Rob's successful sitcom *All in the Family,* and many other classics like *Sanford and Son, One Day at a Time, The Jeffersons, Good Times, Archie Bunker's Place* and *Maude*), to ask if he might produce the film. Lear read the script and immediately agreed to finance the movie. The project was to be the second feature at Lear's new company, Act III Communications, the first being *Stand by Me.* Lear's only prerequisite was that the movie had to have a distribution deal at a major studio, otherwise he would be out of pocket for possibly the most expensive independent movie ever. To everyone's relief Rob then successfully pitched the project back to 20th Century Fox. And, after a few false starts, Fox

ROB REINER

So I went with Andy to Bill's apartment in New York and he opened the door and said, "This is my favorite thing I've ever written in my life. I want it on my tombstone." And essentially the subtext was "What are you going to do to it?" And so we went into his den and we talked through what I felt should be done with the material. I had read one of the screenplays and I thought they'd gotten so far away from the book that they didn't really capture the feeling of the novel. Bill was writing some notes down, and I didn't know if he liked what I was saying or not but about halfway through the meeting he gets up and goes to the kitchen to get something to drink and I turn to Andy and I say, "Geez, I don't know. I hope this is going okay." I just had no idea. And then Bill comes back into the room, and he goes, "Well, I just think this is going great!" He was so excited about my take on it, and I remember leaving his apartment like I was walking on air! I thought, My God, this is like the greatest! This guy that I admired so much was basically giving me a stamp of approval to go ahead. So then we went to get all the financing together and we got it made. But to me, the highlight of my career was getting William Goldman to agree to let me do this thing.

WILLIAM GOLDMAN

They came to my apartment and we met for a while. Rob had done some terrific movies that I liked. I mean, he wasn't Alfred Hitchcock, but he's a great director. And I liked him personally. You don't get offered that many things by good directors.

reluctantly agreed to distribute the film, whereupon Rob immediately set about the task of assembling a cast.

The first people Rob hired were his buddies for two of the pivotal roles: Billy Crystal as Miracle Max and Chris Guest as Count Rugen. Of course, this wasn't just a case of nepotism. Chris Guest was coming off his genius performance as Nigel Tufnel, the dim but lovable metal guitarist in *Spinal Tap*. He and Billy were also both stars on *Saturday Night*

Live and Billy himself had starred in one of my favorite American sitcoms, *Soap*.

As a young boy I had traveled on vacation to the States in the '70s with my American stepfather. After my first trip I became fascinated with all things American. There were many things to be excited about, and one of them was TV. You see, in England, we had only two TV channels, whereas in the United States the cable explosion was just under way. As soon as I arrived I devoured everything related to American TV pop culture, but I became especially fascinated with television sitcoms in particular—*The Dick Van Dyke Show*, *M*A*S*H**, *Gilligan's Island*, *The Brady Bunch*, and later on things like *Soap* and *Taxi*—essentially all the classic shows from the Golden Age of television in the '60s and '70s. Including, of course, all of Norman Lear's shows. I had also listened to stand-up comedians from my stepfather's record collection, becoming familiar with the likes of Bob Newhart, Woody Allen, Richard Pryor, and Jonathan Winters.

So when I got the call that Rob was coming to see me, I'm not sure what made me more excited: that I was about to meet one of Hollywood's most talented young directors, or that I was going to meet one of my TV idols. I understood exactly what was at stake in this meeting. There was no disputing the impact this role could have on my career.

As is often the case when meeting with a director, I knew that I was under consideration, but I didn't have any idea whether I was a frontrunner or merely one of many candidates vying for the role.

A German-sounding voice came over the phone from the front desk: "Zere are two gentlemen in the lobby here for you. Shall I send them up?" Rob and Andy had arrived.

"Yes. Send them up, please," I said, hanging up.

What surprised me as I opened the door a few minutes later were two of the biggest smiles I had seen in a long time greeting me. There

ROB REINER

Well, I try to get people who I know can do a part. I wouldn't just hire friends for the sake of hiring friends. But if they're right for the part, absolutely. The problem I had with *The Princess Bride* was that I had to get a young, dashing, swashbuckling kid, and a young girl to play opposite him. Oh, and a giant. So it wasn't like I had a lot of friends that could fit those bills. I believe there was only one person that could play each of those parts. The movie has that kind of formal English, fairy-tale feel to it—that "In the days of yore" kind of thing. And so I wanted them to have an English accent. At least Westley and Buttercup . . . Prince Humperdinck and Count Rugen and so on. I had seen Cary in *Lady Jane*, but that picture wasn't a comedy. I thought, He certainly looks right. He resembles a young Douglas Fairbanks Jr., and he's so handsome and he's a terrific actor. But I didn't know if he was funny, and this is like a very specialized kind of acting, where you have to kind of be very real and earnest, but at the same time there's a slight tongue-in-cheek thing happening. You have to strike the balance. So we flew over to Germany, where Cary was filming a movie.

he was: the man who had created Marty DiBergi and Meathead—in my hotel room! The other smile belonged to his best friend and producing partner, Andy Scheinman, about half Rob's size but with twice the energy.

What struck me about these guys was their beautiful friendship. They seemed to finish each other's sentences. I was immediately taken not only with their personal charm, which was considerable, but also with their passion for the project. Rob was not only legitimately funny (which is hardly surprising, since his father is Carl Reiner) but also very sweet, with an infectious laugh that could be heard in Detroit, as I like to say. In fact, the man I met was far from the beleaguered son-in-law of Archie Bunker. And man, was he a born storyteller. He was clearly very intelligent and a voracious reader, which is how he knew of

Goldman's work. As it turns out his father had also given him a copy of *The Princess Bride* to read as a kid—just as my stepfather had done for me.

Now, that didn't exactly make us unique, but it certainly inspired a sense of kinship. I knew the story, and I knew a little about the history behind the attempts to translate it to the screen. I also knew that in the right hands it had the potential to be both hilariously funny and heartwarming. I sensed that Rob, given his body of work and his sensibility, was the right man for the job.

I offered them each a bottle of water from the minibar. I have a distinct recollection of Andy being unnerved by the very prospect of being so close to Chernobyl, that he didn't want to touch anything, let alone drink the water.

"So as you probably know, we're making a movie about *The Princess Bride* and we think you'd make a great Westley," Rob said, after settling into a chair.

Rob has that easy way of getting straight to the point in a funny manner. The "as you probably know" sounded almost lyrical, almost as if he were dragging it out in a singsongy way. I think my response was something fairly innocuous, like "Yeah, I heard. That's great!" In my mind, I was thinking, Please don't make me have to read.

"Well, we're prepping in London already, and we'd like to talk to you about coming on board."

This was getting better by the minute. His demeanor was casual and friendly. He had a wonderful way of putting you at ease, and as we began to chat, my anxiety slowly melted away. Rob seemed surprised to learn that I had spent considerable time in America and was intimately familiar with the world of 1970s television. Here I was, a British actor working on a film in Berlin, and our conversation revolved largely around my recounting favorite episodes of *All in the Family*. We segued into a larger discussion of comedy and pop culture, then Bill Cosby came up and somehow—I don't quite recall how—I found myself doing a Fat Albert impersonation, which Rob seemed to like. I explained to them that I had gone to Sarah Lawrence College, as well as having attended the other prestigious establishments in New York.

We talked about *Saturday Night Live*. Again, Rob seemed pleased that I was such a fan of *SNL*. I didn't understand at the time why this was so important to him, but it wouldn't be long before I'd get the point. I knew a certain look was required for the role of Westley, and I suppose I fit the bill in that regard, but, then, so did a thousand other young actors. But they were also looking for someone with a sense of humor. And maybe I had a chance at being able to make these guys laugh. Which I had surprisingly accomplished with the Fat Albert impression. It was looking good, right up until tragedy struck.

"Look, I already think that you might be the right guy for this," Rob said. "But do you mind if we just read a couple of lines? Just so I can hear it?"

Why? Why did he have to make me read? It was going so well up to that point.

Okay, here goes . . . the moment of truth. Reading the lines. The fact of the matter was that I had gotten more work from straight offers than from auditions. But I couldn't think about that now. I had to put on a brave face.

Rob reached into an envelope he had brought with him and pulled out a copy of the script. He opened it to one of Westley's monologues—the one in which he recounts to Princess Buttercup how he became his alter ego, the Dread Pirate Roberts—and handed it to me.

I cleared my throat and slowly began to read. I was cold and unprepared, but luckily I knew the story and the tone of the novel. I also knew that many of the film's best lines would have to be delivered with a barely perceptible wink.

After just a few sentences, Rob held up a hand.

"Okay, that's enough," he said.

I wondered for a moment whether I had blown it already. I had barely read half a page.

"Really? Are you sure?" I replied.

"Yeah. So how much longer do you have left on this movie?" he asked.

I took a deep breath, trying to hide my excitement.

"A couple of weeks, give or take."

"Perfect," Rob said. "We're going to have a lot of fun making this movie, and hopefully, if the studio agrees, we'd like you to be a part of it."

I stammered out something in response, the basic gist of which was "Yes, I'd love to. Thank you!"

Was that an offer? Oh, my God, I think it was!

But then again, he had said "if the studio agrees." Why would they question Rob Reiner, a man who had already shown great skill at casting his other hit movies? I quickly changed the subject, trying to act as cool as I could. I asked them both when they were headed back to London. Maybe I could get them to stay for dinner and convince them that, even though I knew the reading sucked, I was still the right guy for the part. But Rob replied that they were in fact on their way to Paris that very afternoon. This was a whirlwind trip for him and Andy. It turns out they were in the process of trying to track down a world-famous wrestler for the role of Fezzik. Which is about all they could tell me.

"When we get back, we'll get in touch with your agent, and if all goes well, we'll see if we can work it out," Rob said. "If that's all right with you?"

"If that's all right" with me? Heck, yeah, it's "all right." It could not have been more "all right."

"Of course," I stammered. We shook hands warmly and said our good-byes. And I'm pretty sure I was on the phone with my agent before their elevator even reached the lobby.

"I think I've got this one," I said, out of breath with excitement.

"Okay," Harriet said. "Just sit tight. I'll give them a call."

As soon as I hung up the phone I immediately started having an anxiety attack. Was Rob serious? Maybe he offers roles to all the actors he meets to make them feel better? I felt he was a man who could be taken at face value. Best not to waste energy fretting, I thought. Another role would come along soon enough. But you never can fool yourself. I knew in my heart, this one was different. I really wanted it.

The next morning, Harriet called again.

"Are you sitting down?"

"Yes."

"You got it!" she said. "They offered you the part."

I was speechless. This was no small leap of faith on Rob's part. I was hardly a household name. They could easily have cast any number of recognizable, bankable British actors who probably would have been deemed "right" for the

ANDY SCHEINMAN

Well, every once in a while we've found ourselves in a weird position. There was one woman who didn't even have to read for the part, as she was a well-known actress. She came in for a meeting and said, "I'm prepared, let me read for you." And after she left, Rob said, "Oh no. She can't do this." But he'd already offered her the role!

role. But they chose me. In retrospect, it almost seemed too easy. Certainly, auditions don't always go so smoothly. And sometimes a meeting is just that. Sometimes you get the job. Sometimes you don't. You just never know. I guess Rob knew what he wanted, and I was fortunate enough to be in his field of vision.

ROB REINER

Cary was very funny. He did a Bill Cosby impersonation. I didn't ask him to do that. He was just kind of a naturally funny guy, and I thought, "Wow, this guy could really do it." He was the only guy I saw that I thought could play that part. The same went for Buttercup and Fezzik.

ANDY SCHEINMAN

Casting was interesting. For many of the parts, we didn't have a second choice. We didn't have someone else to choose. We didn't have a second for Buttercup, we didn't have a second for Fezzik—for sure! And we didn't have a second for Westley. If we didn't find those people—I believe the last of whom was Cary—then we didn't have a movie. To say Cary was the last piece of the puzzle isn't quite true. Cary *was* the puzzle. I mean, André was very important, but Cary *was* the movie, you know? And we didn't have anyone. We wanted Errol Flynn, and he had to be funny, which I don't think Errol Flynn was. It's not that you have to be funny, but you have to get the sense of humor. It's not go out and be hysterical, but you have to play the part with a little twinkle in your eye, which Cary pulled off beautifully.

I remember we sat down and Cary opens the script, and he reads maybe four words, and we go, "Well . . . this is the guy." I don't remember exactly how long the meeting was, but it was just like, boom! That's him! Rob does this sometimes, and he's great. I mean, it doesn't happen a lot, quite frankly. But once in a while someone will read, or they'll come in and they'll have worked like all night preparing for this big audition, and they'll be halfway through the second line of a four-page scene, and Rob will say, "That's enough. I don't have to hear anymore. You got it. It's yours."

BILLY CRYSTAL

I remember Rob coming back from Germany and saying, "Wait till you see this guy. He's Douglas Fairbanks Jr. but he's also really funny and he does impressions." He's a very alive guy, Cary. A very alert guy. And, you know, I love that about him. He's always so in tune with what's going on at the moment. When I met him, I got the same feeling as Rob: this guy was in the same ballpark with Fairbanks Jr., a young Errol Flynn; kind of your dashing, sensitive leading man, who also could hurt you if he had to.

As Harriet ran through the details of my deal, I was blown away. I recall telling her to accept the offer right away, before they changed their minds.

✣ 2 ✣

PRE-PRODUCTION AND MEETING BUTTERCUP

Within a few short weeks after wrapping *Maschenka*, I was back home in London, which was also the base for the production of *The Princess Bride*. Much of the crew and some of the cast were already assembling. Indeed, the first cast read-through of the screenplay was only a few days away. Soon after I arrived I got a phone call from the production office. I was instructed to go for a wardrobe fitting with our costume designer, Phyllis Dalton, who had done fantastic work with one of my favorite directors, David Lean, on both *Lawrence of Arabia* and *Doctor Zhivago*, for which she won an Academy Award. One thing I knew for sure was that my costume was going to be first-rate. I was to meet her at Angels, one of the oldest costume houses in London and a perennial Oscar winner for design in that field. When I walked into the lobby, the first thing I noticed was an assortment of ornate costumes elegantly fitted on mannequins. Upon closer inspection I noticed that some of them appeared to be authentic, dating back to the eighteenth century.

Within minutes I found myself in an upstairs office, where Phyllis, a demure and very pleasant lady, politely introduced herself. We sat and drank tea as we chatted about the role for a bit. She then leaned forward and grabbed a portfolio she had on a coffee table nearby and proceeded to show me some of the sketches that she had already done for Westley and the other characters in the movie. It was all very carefully laid out, with each sketch including swatches of the material she wanted to use. From the first glimpse I could tell she had nailed the tone and feel of Goldman's book. The colors, textures, and the look of the materials were beyond what I had imagined. For Humperdinck and Rugen there were fine velvet doublets with intricate embroidery. For the Spaniard, Montoya, there was a mixture of brown burlap and leather. For Buttercup, her main look would be a flowing red floor-length dress, contrasting nicely with the black leather, suede, and cotton of the Man in Black.

After studying them carefully I turned to her and said, "Wow, Phyllis! These are really beautiful."

"Oh, thank you. You know, it's funny . . . I don't really like doing sketches," came the unexpected response.

"Really? But you are so good at it," I blurted out, trying to steer the conversation toward one of my favorite films of all time. "What about *Lawrence*? You must've done a few for that, surely?"

"Oh, that!" she said. "Well, on that one I had to do more sketches than I have ever done before."

"Why?" I inquired.

"Because a lot of the costumes had to be made in Damascus and it was hard to get the tailors over there to do exactly what we wanted."

She then told me she had already put together some rough costumes for Westley and that she'd like to have me try them on so that the seam-stress could make any necessary adjustments. Her assistant then showed me to a dressing room, where hanging on a rack was the costume that would come to be iconic: a pair of black suede pants, black leather boots, a thin black belt, a pair of black lace ruffled shirts, black gloves, and a black mask. It was all very elegant and surprisingly comfortable. I tried on the great, billowing shirt, with its huge sleeves. I had already worn one much like it for *Lady Jane*, so it felt a little familiar. Then the tight-fitting suede pants. And finally the boots.

Once fully dressed, I looked in the mirror. Even without the mask, I knew what it must have felt like for Douglas Fairbanks or Errol Flynn trying on their costumes for the first time on any one of their classic pirate movies. A knock at the door took me out of my reverie.

"Are you decent?" came Phyllis's voice from behind it.

"Yes."

She opened the door, looked at me, and said, "Ahhh . . . that's not bad at all." She stopped to ponder. "But . . . there's something missing."

She then called over her assistant and asked her to go and fetch some black satin. When the assistant returned with the material, Phyllis tied one piece around my head and another around my waist like a sash.

"There," she said, "that's better!"

She then had me try on some temporary masks that she had de-signed, which were in fact not unlike the one worn by Fairbanks in *Zorro*. But none of them fit properly. Phyllis explained that since I would be wearing it throughout much of the film, not only did it have to fit per-fectly but, most of all, it had to be comfortable and that the only way to do that was to take a plaster mold of my head. This is a fairly standard procedure on movie productions that involve action or special effects or superheroes that wear masks, although I hadn't experienced it before.

A seamstress then appeared and began to pin the pants so that they would be even more skintight. I asked Phyllis whether I would be able to put them on without difficulty once they had been sewn. She replied that she would prefer to sew them on each day, but that wouldn't be practical given that I would be doing a lot of stunts in them. And, being suede, they would start to give a little anyway with time, she explained. I joked about knowing how Jim Morrison must've felt wearing his signature skintight leather pants.

I then tried on an outfit made mostly of burlap and thick cotton, which would be Westley's clothes as the infamous Farm Boy. Phyllis told me she had been inspired by paintings by N. C. Wyeth and Bruegel, and they felt very authentic to me, but she wasn't entirely happy.

"No, let's come back to these. You need a hood of some kind."

She said she needed a little more time to figure that out and told me we would have more fittings soon. After a few Polaroid photographs were taken to show Rob, I changed back into my boring old jeans and T-shirt, thanked Phyllis, her assistant, and the seamstress, and headed home. The Man in Black was starting to take shape.

The next day I got another call from the production office and was given instructions about where to get a mold taken of my face. I had to travel to Shepperton Studios, where our production offices were set up, and visit the folks in the special effects (known as "FX") department. Shepperton is located in the county of Surrey, about a half hour or so outside of London, and is generally regarded as one of the great European film studios. From a historical perspective, it's the sort of place that has an almost reverential appeal to most people in the business. Among the movies that have been filmed there are *Lawrence of Arabia, Dr. Strangelove, 2001: A Space Odyssey, The Elephant Man, Star Wars, Alien, Gandhi* . . . to name but a few.

Having worked as a production assistant in my teens, I knew my way around film lots a little bit, but to be here, at the famed Shepperton Studios, as the lead in a major Hollywood movie was a different experience altogether. Map in hand, I walked to one of the "shops" assigned to our FX department on the lot and met with Nick Allder, our special effects supervisor. Nick had a great body of work behind him, having already worked on *Alien* (yes, that was his nasty creature escaping from John Hurt's chest), *The Empire Strikes Back* (for you Jedis reading this, there is a strong *Star Wars* connection to *Princess Bride*, which I will get to later on), *Conan the Barbarian,* and *The Jewel of the Nile.* Nick, a very affable fellow, introduced me to his team, one of whom was already in the process of working on an unfinished animatronic Rodent of Unusual Size (R.O.U.S.)—the one that would end up biting me during our fight in the Fire Swamp. It was made of white foam rubber and had no hair, which made it even more grotesque-looking. You could see all the wires and pulleys attached to electronic servos that allowed the "puppeteer" to move the mouth. Even at this stage it looked very effective and they were proud to show it off to me. As I stared at the giant rat with its dead eyes, I wondered if Bill Goldman had ever experienced the same giant rats I had encountered while living in Manhattan—the ones the size of cats, that make you freeze in your tracks. The kind that are not afraid of human beings and carry themselves with that swagger and give you that look that seems to imply, "Yeah, what are you gonna do about it?"

Nick explained that while the procedure of covering my face with wet plaster of Paris was relatively painless, it could be very tedious, as I would be spending a long time, perhaps an hour, sitting in a chair with my face covered in said plaster. He asked if I was claustrophobic, which was kind of unnerving in and of itself, to which I replied, "No, not really," not having any idea just how claustrophobic this whole process would be. He then said, "We're gonna be covering your whole head but we will provide you with a couple of straws to put up your nose so you can breathe."

Thank God for that!

He continued, "If at any time you feel uncomfortable, can't breathe, or if you are having some kind of panic attack, just make a slashing sign with your hand across your throat and we will begin taking off the plaster."

"Okay," I said, wondering just how many actors had had panic attacks before me.

"Just so you know," Nick went on, "if we do that we will have to repeat the process all over again to get it done."

I replied that I understood.

"Great!" said Nick. "Let's get started, shall we?"

He and his colleagues then proceeded to completely cover my head with Vaseline and then plaster of Paris, and provided me with the aforementioned straws to put in my nostrils for breathing. Claustrophobic would be an understatement, folks. It felt like having your head encased in a suffocating, heavy, oversize pumpkin/helmet made of clay. After an hour or so they were done and the plaster eventually dried. It was then cracked neatly open and removed from my head, and the resulting product was used as a mold.

I was meant to look like a pirate. And not just any pirate, but the Dread Pirate Roberts (loosely based on notorious privateer Bartholomew Roberts), the scourge of the Seven Seas. His identity was supposed to be a secret. And while a leap of faith would be required to presume that the other characters in the film (most notably Buttercup) would not immediately spot the resemblance between Westley and the Man in Black, the audience was free to make the connection (which, of course, they did). Still, it had to look right. Despite going to great lengths to create dozens of perfect masks, the makeup department still wound up having to use dark makeup around my eyes in some scenes to create a seamless transition between mask and skin, much like what I understand they do with all the folks who play Batman.

After I cleaned my face, I was met by a production assistant who told me that Rob wanted to see me in his office. We headed over to the production office following signs reading BUTTERCUP FILMS, LTD and went upstairs. As I walked in, Rob got to his feet from behind his desk and greeted me with that warm smile of his.

"Hey, Cary. How ya doin'?" A usual Rob singsongy refrain.

"Great, thanks."

"Good to see ya." He gave me a bear hug.

It should be noted that all hugs from Rob are bear hugs.

"So . . . how did the face mold go?"

"Weird," I responded.

"I know, right?" He laughed. "Did they stick the straws up your nose?"

"Yes. And I almost threw up through them."

Rob chuckled. "Come on, I wanna show you around."

"We have a great crew," he said. "And I want you to meet them."

It was extremely thoughtful of Rob to extend the invitation; not many directors do that with their actors during preproduction. But Rob was different. I would learn later that he had handpicked nearly every member.

I ended up meeting quite a lot of them that day, from the book-keepers to the folks in the props department and almost everyone in between. Every time we ran into someone, Rob would stop and introduce us, and, with unfailing enthusiasm, say to them, "And this is Cary. He's playing Westley."

In the art department I met our production designer, Norman Garwood, with whom I would end up working on two more movies. Norman is an ebullient, sweet guy and obviously very talented. He had worked on two magnificent Terry Gilliam movies, *Time Bandits* and *Brazil*, and on *The Missionary*, all of them containing one of my favorite comedians, Michael Palin (more about him later). Clearly Norman was a *Monty Python* favorite, which made him perfect for our production in my book, being a Python fan myself. Every inch of the walls was covered in magnificent drawings and paintings of all the sets, from Miracle Max's cabin to Buttercup's suite in Florin castle and from Fred Savage's bedroom to the Pit of Despair. They were simply magical. One could really see the mythology of the film starting to take shape. As I expressed my excitement at the visual imagery surrounding me, Norman suggested to Rob that he take me for a tour of the sets they were already starting to build.

CHRIS SARANDON
The crew was fantastic. The crews I've worked with in England, generally speaking, are just great fun. A lot of them are working-class guys, men and women, and they're just loose. They're fabulous.

"Oh, yeah. You gotta see 'em!" Rob said enthusiastically. "They're really something."

Rob took me back outside and we walked over to H Stage, where carpenters, plasterers, and painters were deep into the process of constructing the set for the Fire Swamp, which was starting to get filled with fake trees, creepers, vines, and giant mushrooms. The detail was extraordinary. I remember turning to Rob and saying, "Wow! It's like *The Wizard of Oz!*"

"Pretty cool, huh?" he replied.

He then took me over to C Stage, and as we walked onto the set

I stood and marveled at the sight of the massive clifftop where the famous duel between Westley and Inigo Montoya would take place. Standing on that soundstage, with its cloudy blue sky backdrop, I felt a palpable sense of . . . not relief, but more like joy. I didn't doubt that Rob could pull this off; I just hadn't envisioned how he would do it. Now it was becoming real. I could tell that this was clearly the most expensive production either of us had ever been involved with, and a lot of its success was riding on whoever was playing Buttercup and that fellow playing Westley.

Gulp!

As we walked back to the production offices, I asked Rob about the rest of the cast. He mentioned that he'd already recruited his friends Billy Crystal and Chris Guest, which was very cool. And that Mandy Patinkin would play Inigo Montoya, the avenging Spaniard. I didn't recall Mandy's body of work at that point but I assumed, given Rob's meticulous casting, that he would be a perfect choice. He then ran through a stellar lineup of talent that they were apparently in negotiations with, including Wally Shawn to play Vizzini.

"Oh, I love him!" I said. "How great is *My Dinner with Andre*?"

"Amazing," Rob said. "And I think we also got Chris Sarandon for Humperdinck and Carol Kane for Miracle Max's wife."

"No way," I responded incredulously.

"How about that for casting?" He was almost as excited as I was.

This was turning out to be a much bigger production than I had initially imagined.

"And we're so lucky. We also found our Buttercup," Rob added. "It took a while, but we found her." I became intrigued by Rob's fascination with his discovery of the "perfect" Buttercup.

"How did you find her?" I asked.

"Turns out the casting director had her picture on the wall the

CHRIS SARANDON
My ex-wife, Susan Sarandon, had done a movie with Robert Redford and Redford at the time owned the film rights to the book. He wanted to make the movie, and he gave a copy of it to her to read. I read it as well, and I just flipped over it. There was such a wonderful combination of adventure, romance, satire, and parody; having fun with different genres. And I just thought, This is amazing. I hope this movie gets made. But of course, years went by and nothing happened. So jump-cut to many years later and suddenly I get a call from one of my agents saying, "Rob Reiner and Bill Goldman want you to read for *The Princess Bride* for the role of Prince Humperdinck," and I went, "Oh, my God. This is a dream come true! I love this book."

CAROL KANE
I was beyond lucky to be a part of this. I got a call from Rob about being in it, and to play Billy's wife. At the time I was doing a play in Williamstown. I don't think I even thought about it much. I just said yes. The idea of being Billy's wife in a big old fairy tale just sort of . . . well, it's not something to think about. You just do it. Then I read the screenplay and I loved it. And then Billy and I got together in my apartment later in LA, and we kind of built ourselves a life, a little backstory for our characters.

whole time. But for some reason we never called her in because we were so busy looking for Brits!"

"Who is she?" I asked curiously.

"Her name is Robin Wright. Have you heard of her?"

I had not, and admitted as much.

Rob nodded. "She's on this TV show *Santa Barbara*—it's a daytime soap. But don't let that fool you, she's amazing. She came in and read for us and just blew us away!" Rob went on. "Wait till you meet her. Oh, my God! You're going to love her."

With that we continued walking down the hall. And just as we turned a corner, less than a minute later, there she was, walking up the stairs.

"Hey, there she is!" Rob called out to her. "Hiya, Robin! I want you to meet someone."

She was tall and willowy, with long blond hair and large, blue, ex-

ROB REINER

I saw hundreds of girls, but they had to be as described in the script: the most beautiful girl in all the land. And she had to have an English accent. And Robin, even though she's American, has an English stepfather, so she came by that very naturally. And she was stunningly beautiful and the right age. She was literally the only one I saw who could play the role.

WILLIAM GOLDMAN

I went out to California because we were trying to find Buttercup. She had to be the most beautiful girl in the world, and all these beautiful girls came in, and they were gorgeous, but they weren't Buttercup. Finally, Rob called and said, "I think I found her," and then Robin came in the room and we talked for a minute and I immediately called Rob and said, "Grab her!" Because she was, as you know, just unbelievable. And she still is.

ANDY SCHEINMAN

Robin was perfect. But you know what? They made her do an extra year on *Santa Barbara* in exchange for giving her time off to do the movie, which I thought was kind of rotten. But she didn't complain. Robin was . . . well . . . I mean she's such a beautiful girl. And the part called for that. But there was a sweetness, too. There are a lot of beautiful women, a lot of beautiful actors, but there aren't a lot of beautiful women who are also really funny. Not that she has to be hysterically funny to play Buttercup, but she has to be able to understand what's funny about the script and the role, and have a great sense of humor.

pressive eyes. In a word: gorgeous. She was also very young, as I'd soon discover, barely twenty, and I felt a small sense of relief that I wouldn't be the youngest person on the movie (not counting Fred Savage).

I'll never forget the first time Rob introduced us. "Cary," he said. "This is Robin. She's playing Buttercup! The girl you're going to fall in love with."

A huge smile formed on her face as she turned to him and said, "Oh, Rob!" as if to say, "Please!" and then she extended her hand to shake mine. "Hi," she said in a very sweet tone. What I said besides "Hi" back I cannot recall. I probably didn't say a great deal, since I felt like I had been poleaxed. I remembered Goldman's description of Buttercup in the book:

She was the most beautiful woman in a hundred years. She didn't seem to care.

And that was exactly true as far as Robin was concerned. It was as if I were looking at a young Grace Kelly. She was *that* beautiful. My awkwardness must've been obvious because Rob gave me a little nudge to the ribs and a grin that seemed to say, "Huh? Am I right or what?"

ROBIN WRIGHT

My theory is that they were so completely tired of meeting girls—I think I was the five-hundredth girl they saw—at that point they were like, "Just cast her! Make her the princess!" They were so stunned, after meeting all the ingénues of Hollywood. That was my lucky fate—they were exhausted.

I do remember Robin mimicking a perfect English accent, something she does remarkably well, and then totally disarming me with a giggle that mushroomed into the most wonderful laugh. I remember thinking to myself, Wow! How many women are that beautiful and that funny as well? I mean, it figures that Rob would find someone talented to play Buttercup, but to have that combination of beauty and comic sensibility . . . that's a rare and wonderful thing.

It turns out Robin had stopped by the studio for her own last-minute costume fittings. I think we ended the conversation with her saying she was really looking forward to working with me and me stammering something hopeless in return, like "Me, too." To use a phrase that would be perfectly appropriate in the fairy-tale realm of *The Princess Bride*, I was smitten. Within a few minutes we had gone our separate ways—Robin off to her fitting, and I back to the production office to sign some paperwork and pick up a copy of the schedule. But, to be honest, I couldn't concentrate on much of anything after that first encounter with Robin. She was the perfect Buttercup in my mind's eye. I couldn't wait to get started.

❖ 3 ❖

THE TABLE READ
AND MEETING FEZZIK

A few days later everyone in the cast gathered for our first table read in the banquet room of the Dorchester Hotel, one of London's oldest and most stylish five-star inns, situated in the elegant Mayfair district where Rob, Andy, and Bill were staying. As I entered the room I looked around and noticed that most of the cast was already there, looking very relaxed. The room was also fully stocked with soft drinks and snacks laid on silver platters, including the hotel's famous watercress and egg sandwiches. At the center of the room was a large oak table with some twenty chairs around it. On the table were a number of scripts. A couple dozen more chairs ringed the perimeter—seating for the heads of various departments. I saw Rob and Andy talking to a man whom I immediately recognized as Bill Goldman and made a beeline for them.

"Hey, Cary," said Rob, giving me another bear hug, "have you met Bill yet?"

"N-no," I stammered. "Hi." There he was. Standing right in front of me . . . the legendary William Goldman. A man whose work had enthralled me as a kid. He was tall and thin, and had wisps of gray hair. He also had a warm smile and an easy demeanor about him.

"Nice to meet you," he said, shaking my perspiring hand.

As I began to tell him how much I enjoyed the script and the book—dialogue I am sure Goldman was well used to by this point in his career—the topic came around to Fezzik.

"So who's playing him?" I asked.

"Oh, man. We got *the* perfect guy," Rob said excitedly. "Remember the wrestler I told you about in Berlin? His name is André the Giant."

"His last name is really 'The Giant'?"

"You never heard of him?" Bill Goldman asked, cracking a smile.

"I think I'd remember that name."

"Oh, he's terrific. He's a world-famous wrestler!" Bill replied. Turns out he was a self-described "lunatic fan" of André's.

"Did you ever see that episode of *The Six Million Dollar Man* where he meets Bigfoot?" Rob asked me.

"I think so," I said as it started to dawn on me. "I'm not sure."

"Anyway, that's him! The Bigfoot guy!" exclaimed Rob.

"And it was perfect

WILLIAM GOLDMAN

I knew I had a giant in the story. And then I was watching television once, years before I ever wrote the screenplay, and I thought, André could play the giant. Then I went to Madison Square Garden and I saw him and fell in love with him like everybody did. And he was wonderful for us.

ANDY SCHEINMAN

Finding André was interesting. You know, there's a scene where Westley rides on Fezzik's back while they're wrestling, right? Well, I ended up riding on the backs of so many gigantic people trying to find this guy because when we'd meet and ask them to read, they all said, "I could do it better if you were on my back for this scene." There was the guy who won the World's Strongest Man contest, and I'm riding around on his back while he's trying to say his lines. We met a couple of other guys, including Richard Kiel, who had played Jaws in the James Bond movies *The Spy Who Loved Me* and *Moonraker*. But none of them were right.

ROB REINER

Bill Goldman was the one who said, "You should look at André the Giant." We all knew André because we'd seen him wrestling. But I had no idea if he could act or not. We met him at a hotel in Paris, and when we walked in, the manager said, "There's a man waiting for you at the bar." So we walked into the bar and it was literally like Fezzik was described in the book. It was like a landmass sitting on a barstool. He came up to our hotel room to read. We had a three-page scene for him to audition with, and I didn't understand a word he said. Also, he'd never been in one place for more than two weeks; he was always traveling all over the world. So I said, "You know this is fifteen weeks, right, André? You'll be in town for fifteen weeks." And he says, "I do it, boss." Then he says, "You want me to play these three pages for fifteen weeks?" He thought that was his whole part. So I said, "No, no, you're all throughout the film. There's a lot of scenes." And again he says, "I do it, boss." So he leaves—and he was a really sweet guy—and I turn to Andy and say, "Oh, my God. I don't know if he can do this or not." But he was perfect for the part. He looked exactly right.

casting as his feet really are big," Andy chimed in with a hilarious understatement.

"So he's a real giant, then?" I asked.

"He's literally the biggest guy on the planet. And you get to fight him! How about that?" Rob said with a huge laugh.

The biggest guy on the planet?

I tried to conjure up an image in my head.

At that very moment the door to the ornate room opened and in walked the giant himself . . . André. It was like a scene from an old Western, where the guy enters the saloon and everyone stops what they are doing, including the piano player. The first thing I remember about him, besides his immense height, of course, was his beautiful, sweet, beaming smile. It was a *giant* smile, and the reason for this was because his teeth were regular size, so you could see all of them as he opened his mouth. He had to bow down low as he came through the doorway so that he wouldn't crack his head on the doorframe—obviously something he had become accustomed to over the years. I remember Rob introducing us, and watching my fingers disappear as we shook hands, completely engulfed by a palm bigger than a catcher's mitt. If you want to get a sense of just how big they were google "André the Giant" and "beer can" and you'll understand what I'm talking about. According to his official website, his shoe size was twenty-four and his wrist was nearly a foot in circumference. Standing next to him, I only came up to his belly button!

In retrospect, André seemed to have been born to play the role— like Rob said, "It's not like you put out a casting call for a giant and get a ton of callbacks." He was a real giant, standing seven feet four inches tall and weighing 540 pounds. According to Rob, André had at first expressed trepidation about being in the film. Being French (his real name is André René Roussimoff), he was apparently highly insecure about his ability to speak English fluently. Rob eased his concerns by sending him an audio-taped version of the scene he wanted him to look at involving Fezzik so André could listen to it and study it, and then, if he was so inclined, read for the part. Which he did for Rob and Andy when they flew to Paris after meeting with me in Berlin. When the reading was over Rob turned to him and said, "That was great, André. You got it, buddy!"

"Thanks, boss," came the reply. It should be noted that despite his gargantuan size André took to calling everyone "boss" as a way of disarming them in a very charming way.

Eventually the whole script was put on tape for him so that he could understand and memorize his role. And he did a great job with it, despite English not being his first language and his not being in the best of health. He was apparently due for an operation on his back.

That first table read was an extraordinary experience. There seemed to be so many gifted people in one room. On more than one occasion, I had to choke back nerves provoked by working with such an extraordinary group of talented people. I looked at Chris Sarandon and thought, This is the guy who was nominated for an Academy Award for his portrayal of Leon, his very first film role, in one of my favorite Sidney Lumet movies, *Dog Day Afternoon*.

ROB REINER

So what I did was put down on tape his entire part. I acted it out for him and he studied it over and over and he got it. I mean, we never had to even loop him. So André was the third piece. If I don't get any one of them, I can't make the movie.

ANDY SCHEINMAN

So Rob and I ended up recording all of André's scenes on tape. Rob did André and I did whoever else was in the scene. And André would walk around in headphones, with that tape playing all the time. Listening, figuring it out. And it worked! He was great.

I looked over and saw Wally Shawn, and I instantly thought not only of his remarkable performance and wonderful writing in *My Dinner with Andre* but his roles in *All That Jazz* and *Manhattan*.

CHRIS SARANDON

The audition went something like this: I walk in the door and Rob and Bill Goldman were both very lovely and friendly. And I said, "I'm sorry, I can't hold myself back. The Knicks drafted so-and-so!" Bill Goldman and I then proceeded to talk about the Knicks draft choice for like the next ten or fifteen minutes. Both of us being totally pissed off. By the end of that conversation, I felt totally comfortable because it was just a couple of New York guys talking about basketball. And then Rob said to me, "Would you mind reading the scene?" So I read, and it was the scene in which Humperdinck asks Buttercup if she would consider him as an alternative to suicide. I think they chose that scene because it's very funny, but I read it totally straight. And Rob just cracked up because . . . well, first of all he's the greatest audience in the world. And the next thing I knew, I was on a plane to England to make the movie!

And there was Mandy, whom I now recognized from Miloš Forman's *Ragtime*, standing in the corner chatting with Chris Guest. Both of them serious veterans of the business. It was crazy! Everyone seemed to have a more prestigious résumé than I did. Even Fred Savage had already managed to cram in an incredible amount of television work by the tender age of ten. This was "not your ordinary Hadassah group," as Goldman once famously put it. Even though I did my best to hide it, I began to develop a slight inferiority complex.

There were other surprises that day, like the unexpected presence of the screenwriter Buck Henry, wearing his trademark baseball cap and glasses. He had nothing to do with *The Princess Bride*, but happened to be in London on other business and was staying in the hotel. Even though I had never met him, I obviously knew his work. Here was a guy whose acting and writing career had already spanned across three decades, from creating *Get Smart* in the mid-1960s with Mel Brooks to writing screenplays for *The Graduate*, *Catch-22*, and *Heaven Can Wait*, among many oth-

ers. He was a friend of
Rob's and a repeat host
of *Saturday Night Live*. I
guess everyone felt that
if Buck wanted to sit
in on the reading, why
the heck not? Clearly he
wasn't there to comment

ROB REINER

I did sense that Mandy was very nervous
about doing the movie, and I had to talk
him off the ledge a couple of times. But I
never had to do that with Cary. He was, you
know, very stiff upper lip, or whatever those
Brits do. He carried it off.

on the screenplay—nobody "punches up" Bill Goldman. I suppose the
thought was that if we could make Buck Henry laugh, chuckle, or even
smile during the read, then maybe we were in good shape.

Ironically—given that our characters were at the center of the story—
Robin and I were the relative newcomers in the group. Even André was a
far more experienced performer than we were. Besides appearing on *The
Six Million Dollar Man*, he had been on a number of TV shows, including
B.J. and the Bear, *The Fall Guy*, and *The Greatest American Hero*, and made an
uncredited appearance as a favor to his friend Arnold Schwarzenegger in
Conan the Destroyer. It could also be said that he was a showman in every
sense of the word. This was a guy, after all, who put on a leotard just
about every night of his life and staged a show for thousands of fans.

Up to that point I had only made British films, and table readings
were not really fashionable in the UK back then. A table reading basically serves a dual purpose: The first is to give everyone a sense of the
rhythm of the script (there is a difference between reading the words
by yourself and hearing them recited aloud by all the actors playing the
roles), and the second, to allow everyone to meet one another in a relaxed, fun atmosphere. Basically, it's a play day, at the end of which, if it's
successful, you can begin to get a sense of the movie in your mind's eye.

After a suitable amount of time had passed, Rob signaled to our
production manager, David Barron, for the proceedings to begin.

CHRIS SARANDON

Cary and Robin were just perfection. They were the perfect physical casting for these two characters. And my recollection of Cary was that I thought this guy is a leading man but he can do so much more. He does dialects and tells great stories. He's a very talented guy. And I think we were all sort of a little smitten with Robin because she was so lovely. There's a sense of mystery with Robin that I think she just has naturally. And so I never for a moment thought, Oh, boy, we're in for it with these two newcomers. I just felt like we all bonded. Plus it's so much easier when you're all together and you become friends on location, because then you trust each other. You know each other really well. You know what you can get away with and what's apropos. You learn to get along.

"Everyone please take a seat," David announced.

We all took our assigned seats around the table—a little placard stating our name in front of each of us. Rob was seated at the head of the table, to his left was Andy, and to his right, Bill Goldman.

"Let's go around the table and introduce ourselves," Rob announced.

"I'm Rob Reiner and I'm the director. Thank you all for being here. I just wanna say how thrilled and excited I am to be making this movie. I know we're gonna have a lot of fun." He paused, then gestured to his left and said, "And this is Andy Scheinman, our producer, who will also be directing second unit. And because Billy and Carol aren't here yet, I will be reading Miracle Max and Andy will be reading Valerie."

Andy then lifted his hand and said, "Hi, I'm Valerie." That got a laugh.

As I would find out later, it is customary at table reads for each person around the table to introduce themselves followed by the character they are playing. I sat next to Robin, number four or five on the list of introductions. I remember feeling my hands start to sweat just thinking about it. I folded them in my lap so that no one would notice. When the appropriate time came, and my heart rate was at an all-time high, I blurted out, "Hi, I'm Cary Elwes. And I'm playing Westley."

I had no idea whether this reading was a test. Suppose they heard my rendition of this character and decided to replace me?

Calm, Cary! Try to remain calm! I kept telling myself.

The only thing that even began to bring my pulse down was watching Bill. If there was one person at the table who appeared to be more nervous than me, it had to have been him. As I would soon discover, his colossal talent notwithstanding, Goldman was a rather famously anxious writer. As I looked over at him, he seemed to be withdrawing into himself, trying to become smaller. When it came his turn to introduce himself, he offered a brief background about how he came to write the book, and how the book became a screenplay. How it had been a true labor of love and a storybook gift to his daughters. How for years he had wondered whether it would ever be adapted to the screen; even whether it *could* be.

He then grew even quieter.

"Please understand that this is a very personal project," Bill said, his voice fading almost to a whisper. "Normally I don't care much for any of my work. But this one is different. It is my favorite thing I've ever written in my life. So if I appear a little nervous, that's the reason." He then thanked Rob and all of us for being there, and assured us that the project was in good hands.

On some deep and profound level, I think the prospect of *The Princess Bride* coming to life must have terrified him. After all, this was clearly the most cherished accomplishment of his artistic life. And I don't think many people in the room knew that it was that personal to him until he mentioned it. In hindsight it made sense that he formed a very close bond with Rob. He didn't want just anyone making the movie. He really wanted it to be done right.

I can only imagine what it must've been like for him—sitting there quietly and listening to other people read the lines he had so meticulously written. To watch the actors bring his words and characters to life and hope and pray to God that it worked. It wasn't just that he wanted the film to be successful; I think he was actually fearful it might fail. I'm sure he was thinking, What if no one laughs at the jokes? Worse yet, what if they laugh in places where they're not supposed to? There are so many ways it could all go wrong. Then, after the last actor announced themselves, Rob started to read from the script.

"*The Princess Bride* by William Goldman . . . Fade in on: a video game on a computer screen . . ."

I looked over at Goldman. From that point on, he just sat quietly, taking it all in. No doubt dissecting every word uttered as he silently turned the pages. Every so often he'd pick up his pencil and scribble something in the margin. I noticed he did it a couple of times while I was reading. Perhaps he was just making a note on the dialogue? I certainly hoped that was the reason. Rob did this as well, but mostly he just laughed a lot.

I should take a moment before continuing to explain to those of you who have not seen the movie or read the book what this extraordinary tale of *The Princess Bride* is about. For those of you who have at least a passing acquaintance with the story or maybe even know it by heart, you may skip ahead if you wish. But for those who haven't, I hereby offer some background. If you don't want a SPOILER ALERT, then perhaps you should watch the movie first before continuing, or skip this section.

So, with sincere apologies to Mr. Goldman, let's begin. In the movie version of *The Princess Bride*, the fairy tale is told within the framework of an elderly grandfather reading a book to his sick grandson. The book the grandfather is reading is entitled *The Princess Bride*, and the grandfather promises him it is filled with action and adventure. But the boy, recoiling at the first "kissing part," thinks he has been hoodwinked into listening to a love story. Eventually he becomes enthralled by the tale and can't wait to find out what happens to Westley and his beloved Buttercup. Westley's first words to her are "As you wish" (which really means "I love you"), and he devotes the entire film, and several years of his life, to the pursuit of making good on that promise.

Fearing that a simple farm boy will never be able to provide adequately for his love, Westley sets off in search of his fortune, intending to return one day and wed Buttercup. Alas, his plans are derailed when his ship is attacked by the Dread Pirate Roberts, who, as legend has it, never takes prisoners alive. Several years pass and Buttercup, although still in love and in mourning for Westley, agrees to marry Prince Humperdinck, the rich and duplicitous heir to the throne of Florin. And here the story becomes thick with plot twists—double crosses and triple crosses that make Goldman's byzantine *Marathon Man* seem almost simplistic by comparison. Prior to the wedding, Buttercup is kidnapped by an unlikely trio of men: Spanish sword master Inigo Montoya, the Sicilian Vizzini, and a giant named Fezzik. Buttercup does not realize that her captors have been hired by Humperdinck, who hopes to blame the kidnapping and eventual killing of Buttercup on his rival country of Guilder, thereby instigating a war between the two. Humperdinck feigns love for Buttercup by setting off with several of his soldiers in pursuit of the captors. At the same time, a mysterious Man in Black also gives chase.

Confusing? It gets better.

The Man in Black pursues the kidnappers as they scale the Cliffs of Insanity. He bests Inigo Montoya in a duel (aka "The Greatest

Swordfight in Modern Times"), but chooses only to knock him out, rather than to kill him. Even more improbably, he emerges victorious in an epic display of hand-to-hand combat with Fezzik, and then outwits Vizzini in a deadly battle of "dizzying" intellect, tricking the arrogant Sicilian into poisoning himself. All of this happens in the first half of the movie and sets the stage for the reunion of Westley and Buttercup. You see, the Man in Black is actually Westley, who was in fact taken prisoner by the Dread Pirate Roberts. When Roberts reached retirement age, Westley, figuring that Buttercup had moved on with her life, took his place. This epic plot twist is revealed as Westley tumbles down the world's longest, steepest hillside, having been shoved by an angry Buttercup.

From that point on, *The Princess Bride* becomes more or less a chase film. A very funny, unusual chase film. Westley and Buttercup endure the Fire Swamp, battling its mini fire volcanoes, quicksand, and a battle with R.O.U.S. They are, however, eventually captured by Humperdinck and the evil six-fingered Count Rugen (who, as it happens, was also responsible for the death of Inigo's father many years earlier; a death Inigo has vowed to avenge). Buttercup barters for Westley's life by agreeing to marry Humperdinck, but the prince breaks his promise and instead of freeing Westley, turns him over to Rugen, who imprisons him in the Pit of Despair and apparently tortures him to death. (By the way, this was the moment in the writing of the book when Bill Goldman told me later he actually broke down and cried, he was so sad about Westley's death. He said he loved the character so much and knew it worked but he was also concerned that he couldn't figure out a way to bring him back. So he shelved the book for a while until he could come up with a solution.)

I say "apparently tortures him to death" because, of course, as any *Princess Bride* fan will tell you, Westley is not really dead. (Note: This was

Bill's brilliant solution and what he calls one of "the high points" of his creative life.) His supposedly lifeless body is taken to Miracle Max and his wife, Valerie, by his new allies, Fezzik and Inigo (who believe the Man in Black is just the man they need in order to successfully storm Humperdinck's castle and confront Count Rugen). Max explains to them that Westley is only "mostly dead." Westley is revived, the castle wall is breached, and Inigo duels and slays Count Rugen, but not before uttering, once again, his character's most famous line—"Hello! My name is Inigo Montoya! You killed my father! Prepare to die!" As Rugen pleads for his life and says he will give Inigo whatever he wants if only he will let the Count live, Inigo kills him with the line "I want my father back, you son of a bitch!"

Meanwhile, Westley, still suffering temporary partial paralysis—a side effect of the giant chocolate-covered miracle pill prescribed by Miracle Max—avoids a duel with Humperdinck and succeeds in tying him to a chair. While Humperdinck wallows in cowardice, Westley and Buttercup leave the castle and ride off triumphantly with Fezzik and Inigo. There is a passing of the torch (or the black mask, as it were, as Inigo weighs an offer to become the new Dread Pirate Roberts), a glorious kiss between Buttercup and Westley, and the presumption of a Happily Ever After ending.

So that, in an egregiously truncated form (again, please forgive me, Bill), is the story of *The Princess Bride*. A story we would spend the better part of four months trying to put on film.

Finally we came to the end of the reading of the script, and the whole room burst into applause. I wasn't sure that applause was a common response following a reading but it seemed appropriate under the circumstances. By any reasonable standard, the event felt like a success. It had been peppered with genuine laughter. Even Buck Henry had chuckled in all the right places (Buck didn't strike me as a real laugh-out-loud kinda guy). Reiner was beaming. Bill was clapping, too, and there was a faint smile on his face. For the rest of us in that room, I think we all knew that we were part of something special. Did we think the movie would become an enduring pop-culture phenomenon? Of course not. But did we feel involved in something truly unique? Definitely. For myself I just felt enormously grateful to be there. To be involved in a project with so many gifted people, not to mention getting to be in a film written by the legendary William Goldman and directed by the remarkable Rob Reiner. Life is good, I thought.

Afterward we made our way to a nearby restaurant where they had set up lunch outside on a back patio. I remember finding myself sitting next to Robin again. What quickly became apparent about her, besides her sense of humor, was how cool she was. She could hang with the guys. She told me about growing up in San Diego. How she had always

CHRIS GUEST

Having read dozens and dozens of scripts, or more, I know there are only a handful of people that I can literally put in a class of great screenwriters. And Bill Goldman is certainly one of them. It's brilliant writing. The dialogue is brilliant, the descriptions are brilliant. It's funny on every level. And there are a lot of really well-drawn characters. From an actor's standpoint, you couldn't possibly ask for more. It's a dream to read a great script and you're lucky if that happens once in your life. This was a rare thing where you trusted the words that you had to say.

MANDY PATINKIN

You know, I was never a great movie connoisseur. I certainly saw *Butch Cassidy and the Sundance Kid*, but I didn't know who Bill Goldman was really. I just read the script and thought, This is great. So I had no outside influences. I just knew I had read something wonderful. Knowing Goldman now, of course, I'd think, Well, obviously it's going to be great.

wanted to be a dancer, then done some modeling and kind of fell into acting. She'd been a leading player on *Santa Barbara* for a couple of years, and she had only one previous movie role, playing a homeless drug addict in *Hollywood Vice Squad*.

I had not yet done any television and remember being fascinated by what it was like for her working on a soap. She explained that she had to learn anywhere from ten to twenty pages of dialogue a day, working with up to three cameras simultaneously, with a different director each episode. That it moved very fast, which forced her to think on her feet as an actor. I also remember her telling me how lucky she felt that the show let her out of her contract to do the movie, as normally they didn't do that. I asked her how she knew how to do a British accent so well. She then proceeded to tell me about her British stepfather who had introduced her to Monty Python at an early age.

An intelligent and beautiful young woman who loves Monty Python playing opposite me as Buttercup? Does it get much better than that? And looking around the table at the talent I was about to work with, I felt blessed to have been given this incredible opportunity.

For most of us the day ended relatively early. Most of us except for André, that is, who, we discovered later, ended up spending the night at the hotel even though he wasn't staying there. André, as I stated earlier, was not at his physical peak. He was in fact suffering. All those years of toting around so much weight had left him with this very painful condition, which had only been exacerbated in the ring. I remember him telling me his opponents rarely held back when jumping up and down on his back or smashing metal chairs on his head, thinking that since he was a giant he could take it. I found out from his friends much later on that his classic one-piece black wrestling outfit was specifically designed to hide a back brace.

André was due to have an operation after he wrapped the movie.

But until then the only medication he could take to deal with the pain was alcohol. Now, if you think André could eat, you should have seen him drink. It was legendary. Word had it that even before he developed the injury he could drink a hundred beers in one sitting. According to some estimates his average daily consumption of alcohol was a case of beer, three bottles of wine, and a couple of bottles of brandy. But what I witnessed was something quite different. At meal times, besides the incredible amount of food he ate, I noticed that rather than using a regular glass, André drank from a beer pitcher, which looked a lot like a regular glass in his hands anyway. In reality it was forty ounces of alcohol, which he nicknamed "The American"—usually some combina-

André with our producer, Andy Scheinman

ANDY SCHEINMAN
One day he came to work and I said, "How are you doing today, André?" He goes, "Oh, not too good, boss." I say, "What's the matter?" He says, "I had a tough night last night. I drank three bottles of cognac and twelve bottles of wine." I said, "Oh my God, did you get sick?" He just smiles and says, "No, no . . . I got a little tipsy, though." That was André.

ROBIN WRIGHT
I remember going to dinner the first time with him and he ordered four or five entrees. I'm not kidding. Three or four appetizers, a couple baskets of bread, and then he's like, I'm ready for seconds. And then dessert. He was a bottomless pit.

tion of hard and soft liquor and whatever else he felt like mixing it with that day. I should point out that not once did I notice any sign of the alcohol affecting him, which made sense given his size. So, kids, don't try this at home or you'll most likely end up in the hospital!

It turns out that same night after the read-through André decided he would sample some of the finest vintage aperitifs and liqueurs from the cellars of the prestigious hotel and ended up closing the bar. When it came to last call he got up to leave but never made it to the front door, instead passing out cold in the lobby. The night porter was called, who in turn summoned security, who in turn rang engineering. Manpower was apparently needed. Yet, despite their valiant efforts, there was simply no waking or even slightly budging what could only be described as an unconscious 500-pound Gulliver spread out on their very ornate carpet. A meeting was held and the wise decision was made to leave him there. It was either that or call the police, but somehow I don't think management wanted the publicity.

For safety purposes, both to protect him and any passersby, they decided to place a small velvet rope barrier around André, who was by now snoring loudly enough to shake the lobby walls. The hope was that he would wake up on his own soon enough. But it was not to be as soon as they had hoped.

The housekeepers who arrived the next morning to vacuum had no idea what to do with the massive, sleeping giant blocking their path and were literally terrified to touch him. Then, sometime around 10:00 a.m., André began to stir and eventually awoke to the sounds of vacuum cleaners and the horrified looks of staff and guests alike. He was un- fazed by all this. He got to his feet, straightened his clothes and hair a little, and headed straight for the front door—his original objective. A cab was called by the startled doorman but the driver took one look at André and refused to take him. Finally a minivan was sent for and André made it home safely. Needless to say, he is now part of the establish- ment's lore.

❖ 4 ❖

"EN GARDE!"

I was not a particularly noteworthy athlete growing up. Like most other schoolboys in the UK, I played soccer, rugby, and cricket, but not well. The only sport I excelled in was long-distance running. And even though I generally tried to stay active physically, my interests from an early age focused more on the arts than athletics. So it was with some trepidation that I began to fully consider the requirements of the part I had been assigned to play.

It wasn't just about having the right "look" or even the proper sense of comic timing. There was a specific physicality to the role as well. And while I was young enough, fairly fit enough, and perhaps even foolish enough to think I could handle almost anything thrown my way, the reality of the situation was something quite different.

I knew I could run through Fire Swamps, wrestle Rodents of Unusual Size, and maybe even fight a giant. But when it came to sword fighting? I have to admit that I simply had no idea of the complexity of the preparation that would be required to perform it adequately. And to be honest, simply "adequate" was not going to cut it. Not for a scene that was described by Goldman himself in the screenplay as the Greatest Swordfight in Modern Times. Goldman had apparently spent months researching sword fighting, and all those references to certain defenses and styles were all based on completely accurate sixteenth- and seventeenth-century techniques by legendary swordsmen. You can still purchase some of the fencing manuals written by them online. Books like *The Academy of the Sword* (1630) by the Flemish master Gerard Thibault d'Anvers. Or *Great Representation of the Art and Use of Fencing*, written by the Italian maestro Ridolfo Capo Ferro and dating back to 1610. And even *Treatise on the Science of Arms with Philosophical Dialogue* by his fellow compatriot—the noted fencer, engineer, mathematician, and architect of the Renaissance—Camillo Agrippa, published in 1553.

Back then I knew who none of these people were or indeed very much about sword fighting at all. I had confessed as much to both Rob and Andy early in the process. And I told them that even though I had taken some minor fencing lessons at acting school, it had been determined by my tutors that this was not something they thought I would ever be able to master. I wasn't just a novice; I was clueless.

"Don't worry," Rob insisted. "You'll be training with the best. It'll be fun!"

Training, with the best!

It always sounds fun in conversation. But the practical reality is something quite different. More like, "Don't worry, you'll be training with the best Sherpa to help you climb Everest!" or "Don't worry, you'll be training with the greatest human cannonball before we fire you out of the cannon." I'd long admired serious athletes, and I always try to treat a challenge as an opportunity. And then I began to think, Wait a minute! How hard could it really be? I'd seen plenty of Errol Flynn and Douglas Fairbanks movies. My developing, inane theory was that if they could do it, so could I. It didn't seem all that difficult. A few quick thrusts, some fancy footwork. More like dancing than combat.

I could handle it, I thought. No problem.

I was, of course, somewhat deluded.

On the same day that I first visited the production offices at Shepperton Studios, I was told I would be contacted by one of the two gentlemen who would be in charge of the fight training and coordinating stunts for the film. Their names were Peter Diamond and Bob Anderson. It shames me somewhat to admit this now, but I had never heard of either of these two men when I received the message that day. I reasoned correctly that Rob knew what he was doing and would only assign such an important task to seriously qualified people.

ROB REINER

Because the swordfight is described as the greatest swordfight in modern history, I wanted to make good on that. I wanted it to be great and I wanted Cary and Mandy to be able to do it. I knew that in all the old Errol Flynn movies, *Captain Blood* and *Robin Hood* and stuff, he only did his sword fighting in the close-ups; for the wide shots they would always get stunt people to do it, and great swordsmen. As a matter of fact, one of the swordsmen that we used, Bob Anderson, doubled for Flynn. He was an Olympic fencer, and he and Peter Diamond were the two guys who constructed this fencing sequence.

That, as it turned out, was an understatement.

Peter Diamond was a good three decades into what is generally regarded as one of the most legendary careers of any stuntman or stunt coordinator in both television and film. As a sword-trainer he had worked with both Errol Flynn and Burt Lancaster. And in the previous decade alone, he had served as stunt coordinator on the original Star Wars trilogy. For you "Wookieepedias" reading this, the Tusken Raider that surprises young Luke Skywalker on the Tatooine cliff top with that horrifying scream? That was Peter. He had also been the stunt arranger and coordinator on movies like *From Russia With Love, Raiders of the Lost Ark,* and *Highlander.* Classically trained at the Royal Academy of Dramatic Arts, Peter had also appeared in front of the camera, not only as a stunt-man but sometimes as an actor as well. That's him as the German soldier Indy notices in his side mirror climbing along the side of the eighty-mile-an-hour speeding truck without a harness in *Raiders.* Peter logged more than a thousand credits before passing away in 2004, at the age of seventy-five. He was vibrant and actively employed until the last year of his life.

Bob Anderson was also a native of England and also something of a national hero, having served in the Royal Marines during World War II and as a representative of Great Britain on the fencing team in the 1952 Summer Olympics in Helsinki. He later became president of the British Academy of Fencing and a coach for the British national team. His expertise as a swordsman eventually took him to Hollywood, where he became a sought-after stuntman and fight coordinator. The man's résumé was breathtaking, from coaching Errol Flynn like Peter in the 1950s to choreographing fight scenes for several James Bond films in the 1960s, and working alongside Peter in *From Russia With Love* and (Star Warrior alert) on the Star Wars trilogy. That is Bob using the dark side of the Force as Vader in all the light-saber sequences. Bob also passed away, in 2012, at the age of ninety, but worked until the last, serving as "sword master" for Peter Jackson's Lord of the Rings trilogy.

There was no Google back then, and in hindsight, I almost think it was better that I was blissfully unaware of the incredible reputations of the two men with whom I would be training. Had I known of their backgrounds, I might have been completely intimidated. But I was curious about the man I would be dueling with. Over drinks after the first table read, I had started to get to know

MANDY PATINKIN

Goldman wrote in the introduction to my character that he is "the world's greatest sword fighter," and I figured, that's what I've got to learn how to do. So I immediately got in touch with Henry Harutunian, who was the Yale fencing coach, and we worked together for two months. He taught me the basics of fencing. I was a righty, and he taught me first how to fence with my left hand; we worked the left before the right, and I actually became a better left-handed fencer than a right-handed fencer.

Mandy a little. At some point the conversation naturally turned to the subject of sword fighting and the preparation we'd both be expected to endure prior to filming. I casually asked him if he had any experience with fencing.

He sort of frowned a little—in much the same way that Inigo Montoya might have done—and said, "Not really."

I breathed a sigh of relief. "Neither have I, really. Just a little at acting school. But I don't remember any of it," I told him.

I figured we'd be going in raw, the two of us. It was only later on that I discovered that he had been training for two months in the US and was thus already way ahead of me in the process.

Looking back, I do believe he was sizing me up from the moment we shook hands, trying to determine if I was someone he could "beat." That's the funny thing about acting: it can be collegial and collaborative, but it can also be intensely competitive. A healthy competition between actors is never a bad thing. As actors you work together, but you also try

ROB REINER

I'm sure there was a sense of competition between Cary and Mandy, and I think that was probably healthy. This is a duel to the death, supposedly, and so it is a competition. I think that was there, for sure.

MANDY PATINKIN

It was 1986. My father died in 1972. I read that script and I wanted to play Inigo because my mind immediately went, If I can get that six-fingered man, then I'll have my father back, in my imaginary world. He'll be alive in my imagination. So that was it for me. It was like, I'll become the greatest sword fighter, and my reward will not be to be in this movie that ended up being what it's become to all these people; my reward will be that my father will come back.

to push each other . . . bring out the best in each other. I knew I would not only have to bring my A-game as an actor on this film but I also had to be on my toes in the duel with this guy. We would, after all, be using swords on the day, not the protected rapiers we would be practicing with.

Having gotten to know Mandy a bit, I can safely say with some assurance that Inigo Montoya was indeed the perfect role for him; he was born to play it. Like Inigo, Mandy was passionate and ambitious, if not a little competitive. Even today, when you watch him perform, you can tell that here is an actor who still has splinters in his feet from all the years treading the boards on Broadway. That is where he honed his confidence and professionalism—from performing live on a stage literally thousands of times. And there's no question that some of the best actors have honed their skills in the theater. Mandy certainly fell into that category.

By the time I met him, he'd already been established as a uniquely

ROB REINER

Mandy is a great actor, but you know, every actor is insecure. I didn't see Cary's insecurity but he obviously had it. I don't know any actor that isn't insecure. With Mandy, though, at that time he would carry his insecurities on his sleeve. It would be out there. He had done *Evita* and *Sunday in the Park with George*, he had won a Tony, and he's a brilliant actor, extremely talented. But he'd worked on *Heartburn*, and they replaced him with Jack Nicholson and he was all worried that he wasn't going to do well in *The Princess Bride*. He wanted it to be perfect, and after one of the first days of shooting, I went into the trailer with him and I said, "Mandy, you don't have to do anything. You are so talented you don't have to try; just get out of your own way. You've got great words to say, you're a brilliant actor, and you just let them come out and you're going to be great." And from then on he was cool.

versatile performer, having starred not only in *Ragtime* but also in *Yentl* (for which he was nominated for a Golden Globe). He had also received a Tony Award for his role as Che Guevara in Andrew Lloyd Webber's *Evita* in 1979. You don't build a body of work like that without a significant degree of talent and ambition. Mandy had both in abundance. Looking back, it's hard to imagine anyone else playing Inigo Montoya. He seized the role and made it his own, embracing it with a zeal and intensity that would have made the Montoya family proud.

So I had a formidable foe in Inigo. That much was obvious the moment we began training for the dueling sequence, which for us began almost immediately. The very next morning after the table reading, I got a very early call from one of the trainers.

"Good morning, Cary. This is Peter Diamond," came the voice on the other end. "Are you ready to do some sword fighting?"

"Absolutely," I said enthusiastically, if a little groggily.

"I have to ask before we start . . . have you had any training?"

I shared once again about my amateur skills honed at acting school.

"Do you remember any of it?"

"Um . . . no. Not really."

"Right. That's no problem. Probably better, actually," came the response.

"What do I need to bring?" I inquired.

"Sweats, sneakers, and a T-shirt," he said.

"That's it? Nothing else?"

"No, just be ready to work. We'll break for a quick lunch, but basically we're going to be training from nine to five, five days a week."

I thought about that for a moment. Eight hours a day? That meant forty hours a week.

MANDY PATINKIN

I remember Rob saying to me that these guys, meaning the characters in the film, are holding poker hands, but they just kind of hide it. Then he held up an imaginary hand of cards at the table, and sort of turned his hand around as though he was hiding the cards in his pocket, and he said, "Every now and then, one of these guys shows his cards." And I remember that image of hiding your hand, and letting one of the cards peek out every now and then, meaning a smile, or something that you were hiding. The sense of humor about it, a little bit of tongue-in-cheek-ness.

"Seriously?" I asked half jokingly.

There was a pause on the other end of the line.

"Oh, yes, Cary. We've got a lot of work to do," he replied in a no-nonsense manner. "We start tomorrow bright and early. Nine a.m. sharp."

He then gave me the details of where to meet. I jotted it down on a notepad, we said our good-byes, and I hung up the phone. I had no idea what to expect. I still hadn't figured out that he and Bob Anderson were not merely stuntmen but the finest sword-trainers available. Nor had I fully grasped the concept of a forty-hour workweek devoted entirely to becoming proficient in an athletic endeavor. To put it mildly, it was a little more than I had bargained for.

The next day I arrived promptly at 9:00 a.m., as requested, at a dance studio the production had rented for us off Oxford Street in Soho. As I walked through the door, I immediately noticed that Mandy was already there, sword in hand, his breathing labored and his face glistening with sweat; it was obvious he'd been there for some time.

Damn you, Inigo!

I introduced myself to Peter and Bob. In all candor, my first thought was, Wow! They really picked some old-timers to work with us. But boy, was I wrong. At five foot six, Peter may have been a short, barrel-chested man with thick arms, big hands, rosy cheeks, and an easy, jovial smile; but at fifty-seven he was still in peak physical condition and tough as nails, too. He had an air of athleticism and physicality. You just knew that he could take care of himself in almost any situation and could easily disarm anybody within a nanosecond, with or without a weapon in his hand. I once saw him demonstrate it in a bar, all the while holding a beer in one hand without spilling a drop.

By contrast physically, Bob was tall and lithe, perhaps six feet, and equally impressive, but in a different sort of way. He had the stature that you'd expect in a fencer. And, even at the age of sixty-four, he was just as light on his feet as Peter and as insanely flexible and proficient with a blade. Both were fitter than most men less than half their ages. Which was precisely my demographic.

Nervous much?

Bob proceeded to explain to Mandy and me that the most efficient use of his and Peter's time would be to split their tutorial efforts: I would be working with Peter, while Mandy would be working with him. He then asked me a few basic questions about fencing and swordsmanship, none of which I could answer. Mandy, it turns out, could, having already started his training in the US.

Damn you again, Inigo!

"Okay," Peter said. "Both of you, pick up a sword. First things first. You need to know how to hold it properly."

We did as instructed. I looked out of the corner of my eye at Mandy, who clearly appeared far more comfortable than I did.

"Like this," Peter said, demonstrating to both of us, but looking at me. "'Not too tightly, not too lightly' is the phrase to remember."

He adjusted my grip.

The sword, a light rapier, felt foreign in my hand, and surprisingly awkward.

MANDY PATINKIN

I went to London and began working with Bob Anderson, training religiously with him every day. Cary and I were in different scenes often, so he would be filming and I would be free to train with Bob for eight to ten hours a day, and then I would be filming and Cary would be free to train eight to ten hours a day. We'd meet each other at lunchtime to practice together. And we did this for four months of the filming, and all the fencing sequences for the most part were placed toward the end of the movie so that we would have the optimum amount of time to prepare.

"Think of it like you're holding a bird in your hand," Peter said. "If you hold it too tightly, you'll strangle it. Too loosely, and it'll fly away." Then, as if to prove his point, Peter tapped my sword faster than lightning with his blade—so fast I barely saw it move—causing it to fall out of my hand and land with a clatter on the floor.

"See?" he said with a smile.

"Yes."

The answer, of course, was really "No." I hadn't even seen it coming.

I was instantly transfixed by the skill and expertise of these guys. I only hoped that I could live up to their expectations.

Peter then adjusted Mandy's grip, ever so slightly.

"Ah, yes," he said. "You've done a little of this, I see."

Mandy sort of shrugged. No big deal for him. The novice in the room had already been spotted.

And then we went to work. The first day was devoted to the most basic body mechanics, starting with the proper stance. Mastery wasn't really the goal—there wasn't enough time for that. Rather, it would have to be the illusion of mastery, and that could only be achieved by adhering to the fundamentals of fencing: how to stand, where to place your arms and feet. How to hold your free hand, not clenched but relaxed (something I had a hard time perfecting). A professional fencer, they explained, could watch a sword-fighting sequence on film and tell immediately if the actors involved were complete amateurs. The easiest to spot were when the actors or stuntmen could be seen just hitting the swords back and forth, over and over in the same manner, the way kids do with sticks.

They explained that they had requested that the fighting sequences be filmed late in the production, allowing us a few weeks of intense daily training in prep, followed by a few months of training while on location. Bob then pointed out that although it wasn't possible for either of us to become an Olympic-caliber fencer in that amount of time, maybe with the help and guidance of both himself and Peter, we might just be capable of fooling all but the most discerning of viewers. Their reputations were at stake as well, after all, he pointed out.

Learning the posture of fencing is rather like calisthenics, they explained. You have to have very strong legs, and in particular thighs, as it's your thighs you have to train to get the stance correctly. If you don't, then all of it just turns to mush, Peter said. You have to rest on your haunches, with your knees slightly bent at all times but with your back straight and your legs spread apart—one foot facing one way and the other foot facing the other—so that you're able to go backward and forward at any given time. Almost like a crab. And it's far more stiff and uncomfortable than you might imagine.

By noon on the first day I was silently screaming in my head for a lunch break, and not because I was particularly hungry but because the muscles in my very core, ones I didn't even know I possessed, throbbed in agony. I was covered in sweat in no time; Mandy only slightly less so.

"Keep your left hand up in the air," Peter said, referring to my free hand. "Your right wrist has to be relaxed and free. You should never be tense. If you feel tense, you will look tense."

I listened carefully and tried to follow every direction, but as any athlete can tell you, things begin to break down when the mind is willing but the body unable. My abdominal muscles cried out in pain, as if I'd done a thousand sit-ups. My calves and thighs burned as if I had climbed a hundred stairs. "Back and forth, back and forth," Peter instructed. I scurried across the room, shuffling awkwardly from one wall to the other. The idea was simply to become acquainted with the motion. I was told not to worry about the sword so much at this point, to just hold it aloft and not even think about doing anything with it for now—all of that would come later. The weapon, they explained, would eventually become an extension of my arm. Of course, merely holding the sword for that amount of time was exhausting. Every couple minutes Peter would tell me to stop and adjust my grip or stance. Then we'd do it some more.

Later that afternoon, we were treated to a rather extraordinary little show.

"We're going to show you what fencing really looks like," Bob said.

Mandy and I were ordered to the side of the studio while he and Peter took positions opposite one another and began to duel. It was an incredible sight to behold! They moved at lightning speed. And the fact that they waited until we were both tired and feeling utterly inept was a stroke of professorial genius, as it greatly enhanced our appreciation for the skill and dexterity on display. Had their demonstration come at the beginning of the day, before I'd had an opportunity to fumble around a bit with the weaponry, I might not have fully appreciated what I was seeing. But now, while my muscles were aching and my frustration building, I could not possibly have been more impressed.

I looked at Mandy. He looked back and smiled. Very quietly, I mouthed, "Wow!" He nodded in agreement.

I think we may have even applauded when they finished. Bob then explained that what we had just witnessed was a finely tuned version of the first of many sequences they hoped to teach us.

The first of many? How many?

"Here's what we're going to do," Bob said, looking at me. "After we train you for a while, we're going to flip it around and I'll teach you Mandy's moves."

Hmmmmmmmm. Okay . . .

"Then Peter is going to go teach Mandy all of your moves. You are basically going to learn each other's moves, as well, so there can be no room for error."

Another pause. A hard look in the eye, teacher to student.

"All clear?"

Again I looked at Mandy. We nodded in unison.

The amount of creative freedom that had been given to Bob and Peter was both remarkable and logical. Apart from the statement by Goldman that this was to be the Greatest Swordfight in Modern Times, and the references to the period techniques, there was in fact limited stage direction in his script while Westley and Inigo clamber up and down rocks and engage in witty repartee.

With those six words as their guiding principle (and keeping in mind the twist at the middle where both combatants reveal that they had been dueling with their weaker hands), Peter and Bob had virtually free rein to choreograph a fight that would hopefully be remembered as one of the best ever put on the silver screen.

Fortunately, they were more than up to the task.

Over lunch that day we chatted about movies and the role of stunt-men and stunt coordinators. That was when Mandy and I began to learn of their past work on film and TV. As Bob and Peter related tales of working with Errol Flynn, Burt Lancaster, Sean Connery, Alec Guinness, and Harrison Ford, our enthusiasm and respect grew immeasurably.

Bob then explained that in order for us to succeed in pulling off the sequence, the duel had to be convincing from both an aesthetic and athletic standpoint. In short, it had to look like the real deal. He further pointed out that Rob's goal from the very beginning was to film a scene in which the actors themselves appeared in every frame of the fight, as opposed to using stunt doubles. This was ambitious; after all, as Peter pointed out, even Lancaster, Flynn, and Fairbanks on occasion let the real fencing masters do the most challenging work.

Gulp again!

They both suggested we do homework by watching some of the best swashbuckling movies Hollywood had produced, such as *The Black Pirate, The Adventures of Robin Hood, The Sea Hawk,* etc., so that we could study them and absorb the artistry and athleticism.

"And all the while, remember, we're going to do it even better. We're going to create the swordfight to end all swordfights," Bob stated confidently.

"And as we teach you how to fight, as we go through the training, you'll begin to see how they broke down their sequences in those films," Peter explained.

And he was absolutely right. Watching one of these movies prior to training was a completely different experience from watching after we'd begun working with Peter and Bob. I could actually see how and what they had practiced. I could see where they made mistakes and where they sort of flubbed part of the fight. Our assignment was to find these mistakes and point them out to our instructors.

After lunch we went into separate studios, as we would do for the next few weeks before going on location. I practiced with Peter and Mandy with Bob. It was trial and error, starting and stopping each time I made a mistake (which was frequently). It was rather like doing a movie scene: if you make a mistake, you stop and go back to the beginning. And Peter made me do it over and over, until I got it right. It was a matter of repetition, like studying lines in a script. There were no shortcuts. One just had to keep working at it until it became second nature.

Scripted fighting is very much like the choreography of a dance: two partners working with each other in an attempt to create something perfectly synchronized. In a scripted fight, though, there is the added element of competition. The audience is supposed to believe that the two combatants are really trying to hurt each other. To that end, the actors must legitimately "fight," all the while knowing how the battle will end.

There are a few very basic, universal moves, and Mandy and I had to learn these first before doing anything else. The first of these was essentially how to defend yourself. For example, to deflect a hit, we had to think of our swords as an extension of our hands. So if I'm looking at my "opponent," and I've got my fist holding the sword directly in front of my face, and my opponent tries to strike the right side of my head as a swipe, as if to cut my neck sideways, my deflective maneuver is to move my arm to the right as the swipe approaches. My sword is then up and effectively blocks my opponent's blade. It looks rather dramatic and potentially lethal, but really all I've done is move my sword a few inches to one side, in anticipation of what I know is coming, much as you would move your arm or hand if someone was trying to hit you from that angle. On the other hand, if my opponent tries to cut my thigh or stomach, instead of moving my fist straight up and to the right, I just flip the sword downward and do the same thing. If he tries to cut my left flank, I move to the left, and so on. Obviously, this takes some coordination to avoid accident or injury, but with time and practice, they assured us, it would become routine. Economy of movement is paramount, they said.

It should all look more dangerous and difficult than it really is.

And so we practiced each one of these maneuvers maybe hundreds of times that very first day.

"Start working your wrist," Peter said after a while. "Remember: be fluid."

MANDY PATINKIN

I recently did a vaudeville show, and there is a language to that, as there is in various sports, and dance, etc. If I do this step, then you do that step. Or we do it together, and you just learn that language. Our swordfight was the same way. You make certain moves toward me, and there are a variety of responses I can make. But it's limited. It's not infinite.

"There is something Zen-like about fencing," he said. "Kind of like letting the sword almost guide you."

"You mean, like 'using the Force'?" I asked, making a reference to his work on that film.

"If you like, yes," came the quick response.

"And always watch your opponent's eyes," he said. "Don't look at his sword. If you watch his sword, you'll make a mistake. If you watch his eyes, however, you will know what his next maneuver is going to be, as he will telegraph it." All I could think of was Bruce Lee's line from *Enter the Dragon* when he slaps his student on the head with the warning, "Never take your eyes off your opponent."

I found it interesting that we did not wear protective gear of any sort while we were training: no gloves or chest protectors or face masks. Yes, the tips of our blades were covered, but they were still quite capable of gouging an eye from its socket or injuring you in some fashion if wielded recklessly. To drive that point home, Peter at one point whipped me across the rib cage with his rapier.

I winced, stifling a little whimper.

"Did you feel that?" he asked, although I think he knew the answer.

"A little," I lied.

"Good," he said. "Remember that. That's what can happen if you are not paying attention."

I felt like Grasshopper in the TV series *Kung Fu*. He was right, this *was* very Zen-like training. All joking aside, Peter and Bob were intense and serious about their work. It was clear they weren't messing around. They wanted to make sure that we got the point, so to speak.

As the first day came to a close, with Mandy and I both thoroughly exhausted by this point, our trainers then offered what amounted to an honest assessment.

"Obviously the key moment in the sequence," Bob said, "is when you have to change from being right-handed to left-handed. To be perfectly honest, we're not sure that we can teach you to be left-hand-proficient in time. We just wanted you to know that. We've told that to the producers and to Rob. You can't teach someone to fight left-handed in this short a space of time and have them be totally professional."

He stopped, looked over at Peter.

"So we will probably have to have stunt doubles standing by if need be. Just in case."

In retrospect, I wonder if this was the complete truth, or merely a motivational ploy on their part. Certainly it had the latter effect, particularly on Mandy, who said, almost without hesitation, "Don't worry. We'll get it."

The room was quiet for a moment. Mandy looked at me. What was I going to do? Did I think a stunt double might be necessary to stage "the Greatest Swordfight in Modern Times"? Of course it occurred to me that it might not be a bad idea after Bob had suggested it. Was I going to admit that now, seconds after Mandy had promised no such assistance was necessary?

No frigging way.

"Sure," I said. "We can do it."

That night, as I shuffled around my room on my aching joints and muscles, I wondered what I'd gotten myself into. I could barely fight with my right hand! How the heck was I ever going to learn how to do all this with my left? I could barely walk or lift anything.

The second day of training, less than twelve hours later, was even worse. I spent the whole morning resting on my haunches, trying to ignore the burning in my legs.

"Told you you might be a bit stiff," Peter said with a smile.

About an hour into training, I had stopped focusing on the stiffness and had moved on to severe doubt and dread. Not dread as in Dread Pirate Roberts—but real dread! Fear was creeping in.

Could I really do this?

Even though I had the finest teachers in the world, and a costar whose unwavering commitment pushed me to a level I thought unattainable, I began to realize that the art of fencing is exponentially more difficult to master than it appears to be. And if you are completely new to this, even if you're training several hours a day to achieve at least the appearance of proficiency, it's almost impossible. I don't care if you are the fittest guy on the planet with the dexterity of Yoda.

I may be many things but I am certainly not a quitter. So I kept going to the studio, day after day, and, thankfully, after a while things began to get a little easier. Slowly but surely, my muscles adjusted to the tasks expected of them. Inadequacy began to give way to competency. Peter and Bob broke everything down into minutiae. We'd train and train, learning one sequence at a time. They'd teach us the first five moves, then add another five moves, and then another set . . . and so on and so forth, until we finally had the basic outline of the whole fight.

After a while I started to gain more confidence, perhaps even becoming a little cocky. It's a natural thing, I suppose, in any sporty endeavor, especially one that involves combat. I wanted to show off for my mentors, maybe even prove myself worthy of their respect.

"Come on, show me what you've got," I'd say to Peter. Inevitably, shortly after that brazen comment, there would then be a quick flash of silver, the sound of metal clinking against metal, and I'd be suddenly standing there unarmed, my sword having been swept from my hand and deposited on the floor in what felt like less time than it takes to draw a single breath. As if I needed reminding, this was humbling proof that either one of these men, despite being three decades older, could kick my butt at a moment's notice.

And so it went, for two and a half weeks. Mandy and I could not develop much camaraderie during this time because, for the most part, they kept us separated. Every so often they would bring Mandy into the studio where I was training with Peter and say, "Okay, let's see you try it with each other. Just the first sequence." Then we'd practice a couple times, make a few mistakes, and they'd separate us again.

At the end of each day I would drive home, bathe my aching muscles in a hot bath, have a bite to eat, and work on the script. I'd devoured it cover to cover a few times already, and loved it more and more with each successive reading, but I hadn't really begun memorizing all my lines. I tried a few times, but the day's fencing efforts proved too draining. As soon as I'd curl up on the sofa and begin looking at the words, even with the best intentions, I'd crash having learned only a couple of scenes.

In the last few days before the start of principal photography, Bob and Peter explained that we had only skimmed the surface. The training would go on every day during the shoot. Unlike the other actors, we would not have the luxury of any downtime.

"If you have a single free moment, we're putting a sword in your hand," they promised.

And they weren't kidding. They were on the set every day, lurking in the shadows, waiting for any opportunity to grab Mandy or me. They figured logically that if the fight training was put off until the end of the day's shoot, we'd be too tired to give it much of an effort. So instead, they would stand behind the camera and wait like hawks. As soon as a new setup was called for—which opened a ten-minute window in the schedule—Peter would appear out of nowhere, rapiers in hand.

"C'mon. Let's go. No time to waste."

As a result, Mandy and I hardly ever sat down during the entire production. While the other actors were hanging out and generally having a good time, we were working on our fight sequence—day in and day out. For me, it was the equivalent of a graduate-level course in professional fencing from two masters. I will never forget it, and I am forever grateful.

5

WRESTLING R.O.U.S. IN THE FIRE SWAMP

My first day of filming on *The Princess Bride* was also the first day of shooting: August 18, 1986. Mandy and I had finished training at five o'clock the previous evening and a call sheet was delivered to the dance studio. I remember both of us getting words of encouragement from Bob and Peter as we left that afternoon, as well as assurances that they would be with us both every step of the way over the next few months. On the way back to my hotel I looked over the call sheet and saw there was a 5:45 a.m. pickup to go to the studio. I then looked over the filming schedule. For the first few weeks, Robin and I would be filming the scenes in the Fire Swamp on H Stage at Shepperton, the same set I had already visited with Rob while it was still under construction.

I recall sitting in my hotel room later, going over my scenes for the next day, and feeling just a tad anxious. Even though this wasn't my first studio movie, it was certainly the biggest. A lot was riding on my being able to pull this character off. Yes, I had studied the book ad nauseam, which was now crammed full of my notes. I had also gone over the script and done my usual notations in that, too. Nevertheless, I started feeling a little self-doubt. After all, aren't all actors a bit insecure, as Bill and Rob have stated? So was I suffering from a case of good old-fashioned pregame butterflies? Sure, I'll admit it. And to be fair, it was perfectly understandable given the circumstances. This was probably the most important role of my career. If I screwed it up, it would be a while before I would be offered another.

To quote Mr. Goldman from his book *Which Lie Did I Tell?*, "This is not a book about my neuroses—well, maybe it is—but anyway, I will cut to the chase." I decided to call Rob over at the Dorchester. I knew that chatting with him would put me at ease. Of course, I didn't come right out and admit that I was in any way nervous. Instead, I called under the guise of curiosity.

"Hiya, Cary . . . how're you doin'?"

"Great. Thanks," I said, trying to sound confident even though I don't think he bought it. "How about you?"

"Great. How's the fencing coming along?"

"Good," I said. "Peter and Bob are incredible teachers."

"They're pretty great, aren't they?" Rob said. "We're all very excited to see what you guys have done."

He went on to say that the plan was for Mandy and I to rehearse a version of the duel for him on the actual set once it was completed so we could get a feel for the terrain. That didn't really concern me, though; there were other things on my mind.

"So what can we expect tomorrow?" I asked, getting straight to the point.

"We're starting out with a fairly simple scene," Rob said, his voice brimming with excitement, just like a little kid. "You know, the one where you reveal how you became the Dread Pirate Roberts to Buttercup while you carry her through the swamp. Then all you gotta do is save Robin from the fire."

Hmmmm. Saving Robin from a fire didn't sound all that simple.

"Does that involve stunt work?" I asked.

"There are a couple stunts," Rob went on. "But the stunt guys told me it's all pretty basic stuff."

"Really?"

"Yeah. I mean, like I said, one of them involves some fire, but they've assured me it's no big deal."

"Okay, cool." Which is precisely how I was trying to sound.

"Yeah, and the only other thing is you guys are going to be sinking into some quicksand."

Fire . . . quicksand . . . This was Rob's idea of basic stuff?

"All right. That sounds like fun," I replied, trying to sound as upbeat as possible.

I took a second, then finally let out what was on my mind.

"I just want to make sure I get him right. You know?"

Rob had been down this road enough times himself to recognize the tone of a restless actor when he heard one. I remember he replied in a very compassionate way.

"Cary, you don't have to worry. You're him. You got him, without even knowing it. It's all there inside of you."

Then he said something else I'll never forget about the tone he wanted to strike with the characters.

"The important thing to remember, and this is what I have been telling everybody, is that even though I want you guys to have fun, I don't want you to play it for the laughs, you know what I mean?"

"Yeah. You want us to play it straight."

"Exactly. Because Bill's writing is so brilliant you don't have to tip anything. The words alone will make people laugh. It's all right there on the page. So like I said, you don't have to worry about a thing. Okay? You're gonna be fine. Trust me."

I then thanked him and bid him good night before hanging up. Despite Rob's very honest reassurances, I couldn't help staying up late, poring over the next day's scenes over and over again, making sure that I didn't miss anything. That is, until I finally fell asleep from sheer exhaustion.

The next morning I woke up early and went straight to the studio, eager to get to my first day at work, on time and well-prepared. I was ushered by the first AD into the hair and makeup department, where I met with Lois Burwell, our incredibly talented makeup artist who had worked on a couple of my favorite films, *The Draughtsman's Contract* and *Mona Lisa*, and has since become a personal favorite of Mr. Spielberg's. Lois was going to be applying not only my makeup but also a little fake mustache on me a few weeks into filming. This was something Rob and I had agreed on for the look of Westley—a pencil-thin one, which I told Rob would give him a very Flynn/Fairbanks flair if I could grow it in time. I was able to grow one, but I would have to shave it off, as we were filming the farm boy scenes with Buttercup out of sequence, which called for me to be clean-shaven—thus the need for the fake one.

While Lois was making me up, our equally professional hair stylist, Jan Jamison, who had, incidentally, worked with Mandy on *Yentl*, started applying a small ponytail to the back of my head—another look that Rob and I had discussed for Westley. This process involved using incredibly painful, tiny rubber bands that had to be placed close to my scalp so she could weave the hair in. It wasn't her fault they hurt, though. Jan assured me that, given all the stunt work I would have to do, this "backfall," as it was called, was the only way to apply it to my head.

After getting made up I headed over to my dressing room on the lot. There, hanging on the wall, greeting me as I walked in, was the full Man in Black costume. Leaning on a chair next to it I noticed my actual movie sword for the first time. As I took it out of its scabbard, it glistened in the morning light. It had been designed by a professional sword maker, as had all of the swords in the movie, to Bob and Peter's specifications. I practiced a few moves to get the hang of it. It was beautifully crafted and very lightweight.

Once I finished getting dressed, I checked myself in the mirror in my full outfit one last time. This was it—time to bring the Dread Pirate Roberts to life! I hooked my scabbard to my belt and grabbed my gloves and mask. Before I had a chance for a second thought there was a knock on the door. It was a production assistant, a job I had once held, now there to bring me to the stage. I opened the door and let him in.

"You ready?" he asked.

"Ready as I'll ever be," I replied, grabbing my sides.

Just walking onto the set itself was an incredible experience. I'd never seen such a large crew. All the producers were there, along with the heads of all the departments. Bill Goldman was also there, chatting with one of the producers, Steve Nicolaides. Everything about the setting screamed, "Big-time Hollywood movie." What I felt could be akin to the thrill that perhaps a minor-league baseball player experiences when he's called up to the majors and walks into a 50,000-seat stadium for the first time. I felt a palpable sense of awe and excitement.

In the theater, unlike film you have a sense of the finished product even as you are rehearsing. And you get to tell the entire story every night. Moviemaking is a completely different process. It's about shepherding actors, craftsmen, and technicians—artists all—in the pursuit of a common goal: trying to catch lightning in a bottle. A goal that can seem painfully elusive at times depending on the circumstances. Films are cobbled together over weeks and months, with scenes captured from multiple angles and points of view, and under a myriad of conditions. A single scene or sequence, depending on how large it is, can sometimes take a couple of days to shoot—in some cases weeks, as was the case for the infamous duel and the Fire Swamp. Adding to the disorientation is the fact that nearly everything is filmed out of sequence (ergo the need for my fake mustache!). There can be no doubt that a certain childlike wonder is required to do the job, but actors also need an abundance of patience and flexibility, as things don't always turn out as planned. All I know is that I love working in film. And, aside from being with my family, I wouldn't rather be anywhere else in the world than on a movie set. There really is nothing to compare it to.

Standing across from me, getting wired by the sound department, was Robin, looking radiant as ever in Buttercup's bright red dress. After sharing some very nice compliments about our respective outfits, I, too, began to get wired. This is where the sound department hides a small microphone on your person, much like you see in the movies when the FBI or the police need to have someone "wear a wire" in order to catch the bad guy incriminating himself. The reason for this is so the sound department can pick up even the faintest dialogue that may be too quiet or soft to be picked up by the boom microphone. While Phyllis and the boom operator tried to figure where the best place to hide the mic would be on my costume, I looked around and noticed Goldman standing off to the side of the set . . . all by himself. As at the table reading, he appeared to be even more nervous and excited than I was. More unduly anxious than usual, I should say. I remembered his words at the read-through, where he stated that he might seem a little so because this was his favorite piece of work. I couldn't tell if it was that or maybe it was because it was the first day of shooting. I should point out, though, that this was not Goldman's first time at the rodeo. He had spent some time on the sets of *Marathon Man, Butch Cassidy, All the President's Men,* and *A Bridge Too Far.* However, even though he visited these sets, he never stayed for the whole shoot.

This was not a rare thing in Hollywood back then, or even nowadays. The norm is that unless rewrites are needed on the fly, the screenwriter is rarely invited to the shoot except for perhaps a customary visit to meet everyone. He often ends up watching the rest of the production from afar as his baby is nurtured by someone else. Some directors feel a little insecure about having the writer on location, perhaps fearful that they might be judging their methods or vision. If changes are needed, these directors usually prefer to have the new scenes or lines delivered by e-mail or fax. For some, having a writer on the set is deemed at best a distraction, at worst a nuisance. Some prefer to work with them at arm's length (unless, of course, the director is the writer), allowing the script to morph into something else entirely. And to be fair to those directors, this is not necessarily a bad thing. It's allowing the director to have creative license born of inspiration. I remember a writer who had written big studio movies telling me once: there are three movies when you make a movie—the one you write, the one you guys shoot, and the one the director edits. For some writers this kind of banishment can be considered heresy. For others it's no big deal. Neither one of them is necessarily right or wrong. It's just one of those challenging dynamics: whether the director feels comfortable having the writer around or not. It's really up to their discretion.

Rob adored Bill and had such admiration for his talent that he invited him on the set not just for a visit but for the duration of the production. Indeed we all felt that way about Bill. To us he was such a giant, not only within the industry but also within the artistic community at large, that we were all in awe of him. He was also then and still is a very genteel, big-hearted guy. You'd have to be to write a fairy-tale love story for your kids. So there was never a question about whether he should be there with us or not. This was, after all, his favorite screenplay. Why wouldn't he be invited? Although, I got the distinct sense from him that he really didn't want to be there.

The first scene on the first day was the one in which Westley leads Buttercup through the Fire Swamp, hacking away at vines while relating to both Buttercup and the audience how he came to be the Man in Black. The Fire Swamp, incidentally, is described as follows in the stage directions of Bill's script:

WILLIAM GOLDMAN

I don't like being on set. If you're a screenwriter, it's boring. The words are all done, and they're doing the movie, and your work is done. I don't like being around. I never wanted to direct. I don't know how to talk to actors; most of them are half phony. So I don't like being on a movie set. Never have. I mean, I like being there for the reading, because there is work to be done and you can hear it being performed. But I just don't like being around the shoot. So I wasn't there much. But overall it was still the best experience of my whole life.

It really doesn't look any worse than any other moist, sulfurous, infernal horror you might run across. Great trees block the sun.

And that is exactly what it looked like. It was now completely covered in creepers and vines and had large toadstools and moss-covered rocks all over the place.

My first line of dialogue, describing my thoughts about the swamp to make Buttercup feel secure, was, "You know, it's not that bad. I'm not saying I'd like to build a summer home here, but the trees are actually quite lovely."

I recall not getting it quite right. Rob had a very specific idea about how the words "summer home" should be pronounced and thought I was putting too much emphasis on the second word as opposed to the first.

"It's *summer* home, Cary," Rob said.

"Right—summer *home.*"

"No, try it again. *Summer* home."

We tried a second take. And then something strange happened. Before I even got to finish the line an odd look came across Rob's face from behind the monitor. He turned to Andy Scheinman, lifted off his headphones, and said, "What's that weird noise I can hear?"

Andy removed his headphones as well and shook his head. "I don't know, but I can hear it, too."

"Cut!" Rob yelled.

Rob turned to our sound guy, David John.

"Dave? What's that weird noise?" he asked.

"I don't know, but it has stopped now," came the reply from David.

We rolled again. And once again, right in the middle of a take, Rob yelled, "Cut!"

BILLY CRYSTAL

Rob is incredibly smart about his material, and very freeing for actors to do their best work. He also knows what he wants. He'll say, "I want it the way I like it." He wants it the way he hears it. So the dialogue has a rhythm to it, an inflection, a music to it. And if you don't hit the right notes, you know it. He'll correct you about where the inflection goes and so on. I remember even on *A Few Good Men*, Tom Cruise would go up to him and say, "Tell me it again. Just say it." He'd hear it and go, "I got it." And then do it perfectly, because there's a music to it. If you don't hit the note right, it's going to be a little flat. It's about timing, and Rob has excellent timing. And he loves his actors. He's a very giving director that way.

"What the heck *is* that?" Rob asked again, walking over to the sound cart. Our now frustrated sound man rewound the tape and let them all listen to it again to see if they could decipher what it was and thus, hopefully, where it was coming from.

The tape was played back, and I even got a listen. You could clearly hear what sounded like some sort of strange incantation or chanting of some kind. It was barely audible but it was definitely on the sound track. The ADs spread out and began searching the swamp, listening for the sound. I think it was Rob who eventually discovered Bill standing behind a giant toadstool, rocking back and forth, with his fingers crossed in his mouth, mumbling under his breath.

"Bill, what are you doing?" Rob asked quizzically.

Embarrassed, Bill stammered as he removed his hands from his mouth, "Oh, I'm, er . . . I was just praying. Why?"

"You can't talk on the set, Bill. Not while we're filming. The microphones pick up everything."

Bill lowered his head.

"Oh my gosh! I'm sorry," he said. "I was just a little excited, I guess."

Rob threw an arm around him and pulled him close. "It's okay, Bill. Just relax."

Rob then turned to us and calmly said, "Okay. Let's try it again."

The next two takes were printed but apparently I still could not get the delivery of "summer home" exactly right. When a director gives a line reading to an actor—when he demonstrates precisely how the words should be spoken—it can sometimes be a bit awkward. But Rob's personality is so engaging and his demeanor so unthreatening that he is just naturally able to put an actor at ease. He also knows exactly how it should sound. The next take, I finally got it right.

Afterward I said to Rob, "You know, in England we don't really have summer homes given the climate." He laughed and said, "Yeah, that figures."

For the next sequence in the Fire Swamp, there would be no easing into things. This would be a baptism by fire.

Although the stunts and special effects in *The Princess Bride* were certainly modest by today's standards (and indeed even by the standards of some of the Hollywood blockbusters of the time, e.g., the Star Wars and Indiana Jones trilogies),

ROB REINER

Bill was there during the early scenes. I remember he was freaking out the first day he was there. He would get behind the camera and he'd turn his back and he would kind of cross his fingers. And it was kind of a weird thing, almost like a little kid who was hoping everything would go well.

they nevertheless represented my introduction to the technological possibilities of moviemaking, and the risks and challenges associated with stunt work.

This was the point in the Fire Swamp sequence where Buttercup's dress briefly catches on fire before the flame is extinguished by Westley. It's merely a line in the stage directions and consumes only a few seconds of film, but before we could shoot the scene, several steps had to be taken. First, a fire marshal had to be brought to the set. He would then meet with the stunt coordinator, Peter Diamond, Nick Allder, our FX supervisor, and his special effects crew. This was followed by what is known as a general "safety meeting" with the rest of the crew. Anytime there are firearms, fire, or even a dangerous or semidangerous stunt involved, there is always a safety meeting of this kind. The whole crew gathers around, and usually the first AD explains what the meeting is about. He then introduces everyone to the person in charge of special effects/stunts/firearms, etc., and that person walks everyone through the sequence, detailing both process and all potential safety concerns.

And that is what happened that day as Nick filled us in. We were all then invited to walk around the set as he pointed out various places on the ground through which flames would periodically spurt. Each point had been marked by a bright orange rubber street cone.

"Please make sure that you don't step on any of these gas outlets," he cautioned. "Always walk around them. That's why we have put cones next to each one, so you can all familiarize yourself with where the flames are going to come from. There's another one over there, and there's another there. There are three of them in all and we're going to time these to go off a certain way. Just so you guys will know exactly when the flames are going to spurt we have arranged for the sound of air to be blasted through the pipes containing the gas beforehand as a warning. Okay?"

We all nodded.

"Okay, the last one, right here," he said, pointing to a cone, "is going to be the one that sets fire to Robin's dress."

I looked over at Robin. She betrayed not the slightest bit of concern.

"We've had a special dress made for her," he continued, "that is made out of flame-retardant material." Rob then turned to Robin and said, "Robin, you're okay with this, right?"

I've done enough movies in the last twenty-five years to know that this is always a difficult moment for an actor. Actors nearly always want to appear courageous and committed, willing to do anything for the team. So while it is perfectly acceptable to opt out of a stunt and let the professionals handle it, there is some pressure, mostly internal, to push yourself beyond your normal comfort zone. Typically, the director will follow up after the consultation with the stunt coordinator and special effects experts and the actors, just to make sure everyone is at ease with their respective roles when it comes to the stunt. Certainly that was the case on this occasion, as Rob consulted with both Robin and me about our willingness to do the stunt. But more so with her, seeing as she was the one who was actually going to be set on fire.

"If you don't want to do it, it's totally fine," Rob assured her. "We've got the doubles. So it's okay. We can shoot around you."

Robin looked at me.

I shrugged—if you're game, so am I.

She then turned back to Rob.

"No, I think we can do this."

Rob glanced at me.

"Are you guys sure?"

"Absolutely," I chimed in. "I'll make sure she's safe. Let's give it a shot."

We carefully watched the scene rehearsed with our stunt doubles—Andy Bradford for me, Sue Crossland for Robin—so we could study in detail what would be required of us. As Nick had warned us, each little burst of flame was preceded by a loud *whoosh!* sound as a thick blast of oxygen was shot out of the gas pipe; so we always knew precisely when and where the actual flame would appear. At the appointed time, we watched as Sue's flame-retardant dress caught on fire, and Andy put it out. So from what I could gather Robin was essentially going to be set on fire, and my job was to grab her, move her away from the open flame, and then extinguish the fire on her dress without letting her get burned in any way.

No biggie, right?

"All you have to do is rub the dress together, and the retardant will put out the fire by itself," Nick instructed. "However, if it looks like there's a problem, just step aside immediately and Peter and myself will douse her with the fire extinguisher. We'll be right here next to the camera. It's only a small flame, so it shouldn't spread."

Was I apprehensive about shooting a scene that involved an unstable element on another actor? Especially fire? You bet. It occurred to me that even though Robin was wearing a full layer of fireproof clothing beneath her flame-retardant dress, her face and hands would still be exposed. Interestingly, the stunt coordinators and FX team told her that if anything went wrong, she was to immediately cover her face with her hands, which would have been the natural knee-jerk reaction anyway. Did I do my best to hide my anxiety at being the one to put out the fire on Robin? You bet correctly again.

So we lined up for the shot and Rob yelled, "Action," and I walked Robin past the last fire pit. There was a "whooshing" sound, and then the flame. And it was a pretty large burst of flame, I can tell you. It caught me by surprise. Obviously Robin's dress immediately caught fire, but just as I pulled her aside to extinguish it there came a loud yell from behind the camera.

Rob called for cut.

What was the commotion this time? It turns out that even though Bill knew exactly what was going to happen, as he had written this sequence into every version of the screenplay, he had apparently forgotten that this particular stunt was being shot that day and had left the set for some reason, missing the safety meeting, and returned right in the middle of the first take. As soon as he saw Robin on fire he naturally thought there had been some sort of an accident. Thus, he yelled out something to the effect of "OH, MY GOD! HER DRESS IS ON FIRE! SHE'S ON FIRE!!!" effectively ruining another take. After yelling "Cut!" Rob calmly turned to Goldman and said, "Bill, it's supposed to catch on fire, remember?"

Fortunately, everything went smoothly and I was able to put

out the fire without too much difficulty each and every take thereafter. I remember Robin's re-action when the large flame caught on her dress was a very small "Ooh!" rather than a scream, which should tell you just how un-fazed she was by it all. Or just how good an actress she was at hid-ing her fear. As soon as Rob yelled, "Cut," after each take the FX crew and Peter would rush over and douse her with a small fire extinguisher just to be sure. And she would have to change into a succession of dresses once the burn became noticeable.

Bill was so embarrassed at having potentially ruined another take he wanted to book his flight home right away, but Rob convinced him to stay longer. He actually made it to the first day of shooting for the Florin Castle sequences at Haddon Hall before packing his things and leaving. The rea-son I remember is be-cause I brought a video camera to the set that day and shot some behind-the-scenes foot-age that included him. And then, the very next

WILLIAM GOLDMAN

I remember turning to Rob and saying, "You're setting fire to Robin on the first day?! What are you nuts? It's not like we can replace her!"

ROB REINER

We were in the Fire Swamp and shooting the scene where a burst of flame catches Robin's dress on fire. And Bill was really upset, saying, "I can't believe that on the first day of shooting we're setting the lead-ing lady on fire!"

ROBIN WRIGHT

I remember on one take the dress caught fire, and it kept catching fire. Maybe they forgot to put fire retardant on part of the dress. Anyway, it just kept burning. And thankfully Cary put it out just as it was crawling up toward my hair.

day, he left. Just like that. The man responsible for creating this wondrous world, this magical story, was gone. Fortunately he would return later.

Setting fire to Robin was just the first of a couple of challenging physical sequences to be undertaken in the swamp. Before the day ended, there was another meeting with the FX crew, this time to discuss Buttercup's disappearance into what looks like quicksand, referred to as "Snow Sand" in the book, and her subsequent rescue by Westley. Again, the entire sequence was explained and demonstrated by the special effects team and by Peter Diamond in a safety meeting. Located just a few inches beneath the quicksand, we were told, was a trapdoor made out of latex and plywood that was being held in place by a member of the FX team. When Buttercup stepped on the appropriate spot at the appropriate time, the door would be released and she would be sucked into the sand. Shortly after she disappeared, I was to jump in after her, using the same technique. Beneath the trapdoor was a pit filled with foam mattresses to ensure that the person falling down would land safely. Peter and the stunt team assured us they would be down there to catch us and make sure we weren't injured. A marvelous and very effective illusion.

Our doubles, Andy and Sue, began walking us through the stunt effortlessly and safely. As with the fire stunt, they would do one take and then it was to be our turn. In all honesty, this one seemed easy, at least in comparison to the previous stunt. But after watching, there was something about it that seemed a little odd. My initial instructions were to merely walk in after Robin—grab my nose with one hand to prevent sand from getting in it, and jump down feet-first. But when we looked at the scene on playback afterward, it seemed kind of feeble. There was something rather unheroic about jumping into quicksand feet-first. Especially holding one's nose.

"I don't know, guys," I said. "It doesn't exactly seem swashbuckling, does it? What if I were to dive in headfirst?"

Rob agreed, but both he and the stunt team were reluctant to let me, or anyone, for that matter, dive headfirst into the pit. It was much too dangerous. What if I got injured? It hadn't really been designed or tested for that purpose, they reasoned quite correctly. I tried to plead my case. What sort of fairy-tale hero would watch his love tumble into a pit of quicksand, and then take the time to place his sword and sheath on the ground and just sort of step casually into the pit to save her?

No one disputed the idea, but there were legitimate safety concerns and insurance issues that had to be considered. The fear, naturally, was that a mistimed headlong dive into the quicksand could result in serious injury (like a broken neck, spinal injury, or fractured skull) and thus, the termination of the entire movie. There was quite a lot at stake. But then, that's often the case with any special effects or stunt work.

As the relative freshman on the set, it wasn't easy for me to voice my opinion about something that was not just a matter of safety but also a matter of artistic license. But I instinctively knew that stepping into the quicksand didn't seem right, that it wasn't graceful enough to capture the spirit of the story or of the character. I didn't think Westley was the type of person who would be too timid to dive headfirst into quicksand to save his true love. It didn't seem true to his nature. I wanted him to be consistent with Goldman's vision: at once fearless and elegant, romantic and brave. My theory was that if he wasn't afraid to throttle a giant, wrestle humongous rats, and defeat Inigo Montoya in a duel, he shouldn't be afraid to dive headlong into quicksand.

"There's going to be some exciting music here, right?" I asked Rob. "Yeah, sure."

"Then let's give Westley some exciting behavior to go along with it!"

After a lot of beard scratching, Rob finally relented.

"Okay. But not with you, with your stunt double," was his only concession.

This was a big deal for me—it was the first moment in which I felt like a real collaborator in the process, and not merely a hired hand. I had earned the trust and respect of a director I greatly admired.

I pulled Andy Bradford aside.

"Do you think you can do it?"

"Absolutely," he said without hesitation. "No problem." Andy was not someone who showed fear at all.

Peter Diamond then talked Andy through the sequence and how to do it safely. They stood around the pit, miming the dive, discussing proper timing, and then, with the cameras rolling, first Robin disappeared. Then Andy—bless his heart!—after grabbing a piece of vine he had hacked, dove right in after her. He had never practiced the stunt before, and he did it perfectly. The trapdoor opened and he slid smoothly into the sand, looking very heroic in the process.

When he made his way back to the surface with Robin on his back, and using the vine for support, there was big applause from us all. Everyone had become convinced of the merits of diving rather than walking into the quicksand.

"That was great, Andy! Cary, do you think you can do that?" Rob asked excitedly.

"I think so," I replied.

He then turned to Andy. "Can you show him? That was fantastic!"

Andy spit out a few grains of sand and smiled. "Yeah, sure."

Unlike Andy, the special effects folks went along reluctantly. They were naturally nervous that the door might not open at the precise moment. Because if it didn't, I was warned, then I would be smashing my skull against plywood with the full weight of my body.

"Just so you know, guv'nor," they said to Rob, "we're not liable. The trapdoor wasn't intended for this purpose, so we can't be certain it'll work a second time."

Finally, after a practice run with Andy showing me precisely how it was done, it was my turn.

The first AD called, "Turn over," the camera started rolling, and Rob yelled, "Action!"

I watched as Robin disappeared into the quicksand, then I cut a piece of vine, stuck my sword into the ground, took a deep breath, and dove headfirst into the pit after her, just as Andy had done a few minutes earlier. Fortunately, I slid neatly into the pile of foam and was caught below by a very relieved Peter Diamond and Andy Bradford. And I didn't get so much as a bump or a bruise.

After ten days of shooting we were all about ready to leave the Fire Swamp, but we still had one more scene left to do. On the second-to-last day, we were introduced to the little people who would be portraying the Rodents of Unusual Size. In the script there is a protracted and exciting fight scene between Westley and an R.O.U.S. in the Fire Swamp. As opposed to the CGI miracles prevalent in movies

ANDY SCHEINMAN
It turned out much better. But we were scared Cary was going to die. We didn't want him to dive into the sand pit. And even though we rigged this thing with padding, there was cement down there. If he went down and hurt his neck or something, that would have been a disaster. But he did it on the first take, and in the movie it looks fabulous. It definitely helped the movie. It's way more Errol Flynn-y and hero-y to dive than not to dive.

today, we only had a budget that provided for small people wearing rat costumes. One of the little people, Danny Blackner, was from the north of England and had multiple tattoos and earrings all up and down his ears long before it became fashionable, and he looked like a guy who had sprung from the punk rock scene of the late 1970s. I was told that besides being a performer he was also a veteran stuntman, having utilized his skills and diminutive stature to land work in films such as *Labyrinth* and *Return of the Jedi*, in which he played an Ewok. He was an intensely spirited and joyful guy who clearly liked his work.

There were three actors playing R.O.U.S. in all, but Danny was appointed to be the one who would do much of the heavy lifting, and the one I would wrestle with over the course of the next two days. It was no picnic for these guys in the rat suits. First, they were encased in fifty pounds of latex, rubber, and fake fur—roughly half their own body weight. Second, they'd have to use their hands to control the front feet of the rat and their legs to sort of kick with the rear feet in order to maneuver. And third, their vision would be extremely limited.

"This is going to be kind of strange," Peter Diamond explained. "When you fight with them, you'll be using this retractable sword," he said handing it to me, "and Danny is going to pretend to bite you. But don't worry, the teeth are all rubber. It's all fake. Now, the challenge is that Danny won't be able to see much of anything through the suit, so you're going to have to make him move while you're fighting with him. He won't have much of a clue about what's going on."

"Really?"

"Not much, no," Peter responded.

I looked over at Danny, who was still being sewn into his rat costume. He gave me a huge grin and a thumbs-up.

"Just remember, these suits are not very comfortable; it's very hot in there for him. We don't want this to drag on for too long, so try to get it over with as quickly as possible, okay?"

"Sure. No problem."

Since it was getting late, it was decided that we should just rehearse the fight sequence in preparation to shoot it the following morning. So we practiced the wrestling and the bite on the shoulder over and over. We'd always check on the guys inside the R.O.U.S. costumes every few minutes to make sure they weren't percolating. They wore only T-shirts and boxers, but they'd still be drenched with sweat whenever we took a break and they were allowed to remove their giant rat heads.

"You okay in there?" I asked Danny after one rehearsal.

"Yeah, fine, guv'nor," came the usual muffled refrain.

It had to have been sweltering for those guys inside those costumes. There were giant lights illuminating the soundstage, and no air-conditioning that I can recall. I had already soaked through Westley's billowy black shirt, just because of the action under the bright lights, so I can only imagine how unbearable it must have been inside the skin of a 50-pound latex-and-fur-covered R.O.U.S. But there weren't any complaints from the guys in the suits. I won't lie to you, though: as I rolled around on the floor of the swamp, staring into the rubber face of a giant rat, I did find myself thinking, Gosh, I hope this all works out. I mean, the R.O.U.S. didn't really look all that much like fearsome creatures to begin with. Up close, they looked like what they were: little people inside rat suits.

I could only hope that no one would care, that somehow the special effects would seem charming rather than cheesy (which was, thankfully, exactly the way it turned out).

The next day, our final day in the swamp, I arrived on the set to find what appeared to be a large commotion going on. Rob and Andy were

in a serious conference with the ADs and David Barron, our production manager. I approached to inquire what all the fuss was about.

"We lost one of the R.O.U.S.," Rob said.

"What? What happened?" I asked, fearing the worst—maybe an accident or something.

"It's the guy you are supposed to fight with today, Danny. We can't find him."

"What does that mean?"

"Well, we can't finish the sequence without him."

"Can't one of the other guys take his place?"

"No," Andy chimed in, "he's the only trained stuntman. He's the only one qualified to fight with you. It's a union thing."

David Barron looked at his watch.

"If he's not here in the next ten minutes," he said to Rob, "we may have to break for lunch and try and complete this later on."

"But this is our last day on this set. What if he doesn't show?" Rob asked.

"Well, then, I suggest we figure out an alternative," David responded.

After some more consultation with Rob, Andy, and the other ADs,

ROB REINER

The whole thing was a big challenge. We didn't have a big budget—only 16 million bucks. So that was a challenge, just to get all of it done. But the biggest challenge was to strike the right balance in the tone. To be reverent to the genre, but at the same time to be gently satirizing it, which is what we did. To walk that line was tricky. But we had the right people to do it.

ANDY SCHEINMAN

Truthfully, I was a little worried that the Rodents of Unusual Size looked a little corny or weird. But it didn't matter because it was all in the spirit of the film. I don't see Rob as a big techno guy. He's more human. And by that I mean he's more interested in the human end of filmmaking, you know? If we had CGI back then, it's possible the story would have gotten overwhelmed by all that stuff.

it was finally decided that we would have to make do with me wrestling a stuffed rat—the same one that was thrown at me from off camera by Peter Diamond after my line, "Rodents of Unusual Size? I don't think they exist." Believe me when I tell you that wrestling a "rubber rat" felt even sillier than wrestling a little person inside a rat suit. Even Robin was barely able to stifle a laugh during some of the takes.

After shooting what seemed an endless amount of footage of this foolishness (that no one was buying—not even Rob, despite all his positive feedback) word came that Danny had finally arrived on set. We all stopped what we were doing to go and make sure he was all right. There was no question that he was looking a little bedraggled. Now, based on the costly delay, some directors might have sent him packing, or at least given him a good tongue lashing, but not Rob. Compassionate to the core, he reached instead for a logical response.

"How are you? Are you all right?" Rob asked him sincerely.

"I am now," came the reply.

"What the heck happened to you? We were all worried!"

This opened the door for Danny to embark on an extraordinary tale that stopped production in its tracks for the next few minutes.

"Well, guv'nor, it's like this, you see. I had a bit of a rough night . . . a really rough night, actually."

Rob nodded sympathetically and leaned forward. They made quite a pair—Danny, at four feet tall, and Rob more than six feet, with his broad shoulders and thick beard.

Danny hung his head shamefully and went on.

"So I went out to the pub last night with my mates, right? And we tied a few ones on, same as usual. And anyway, when it was time to go home, I got in my special car, you see—"

"A special car?" Rob interjected.

"You know—a car that's specially made for me. See, my feet can't reach the floor of a regular car. I can't use the pedals. So I've got a car that's adjusted for me, so I can drive it with me hands."

By now the whole crew had gathered around. Hanging on every word.

"Well, anyway, such is my luck, I got pulled over, didn't I?"

Rob, of course, asked, "For what?"

"For speeding! Course I wasn't speeding at all 'cos my car can only go so fast, you know."

Rob shook his head out of concern, but some of the crew couldn't help chuckling a little.

"But this copper, he's got another idea. So he pulls me over, knocks on the window, and tells me to get out the vehicle. So I hop off me pile of books—'cos I use a stack of books to get the right height. And I jump out of the car, and I'm a bit wobbly, I won't lie to you. So the policeman, he says to me, 'License and registration.' So I give it to him and he says, 'Do you realize what you were doing?' And I says, 'No, what was I doing?' And he goes, 'You were over the speed limit.' Then he asks me what's the deal with my car, and he wants to know who I am and all that, right? So just as I start to tell him, he cuts me off and says, 'Hold on! Let me smell your breath!' So I give him a quick whiff and he says, 'You've been drinking, haven't you?' And I says, 'Yeah, I've had a couple.' And he says, 'Right, then! Back of the van for you!'"

By this time most of the crew were trying hard not to laugh at this poor guy's misfortune. But Rob remained calm and composed. I think he just wanted to hear the end of the story.

"Then what happened?" Rob asked, genuinely intrigued.

"So I try to tell him he's making a big mistake," Danny continued, becoming more animated as the tale went on. "I says, 'You don't under-stand! I can't go down to the station! I've got an important day's work today.' And the cop says, 'Work?' Just like that—'Work?'—like he don't think I can earn a decent wage or something. 'What do you do for a living?' So I tells him, 'I'm an actor!' right? And he just laughs and says, 'Yeah, right, pull the other one!' And I says, 'No, it's true, officer! I'm an actor and a stuntman and I have to be on the set in a few hours.' Then the cop asks me, 'Okay, what part are you playing?' And I says, 'I'm play-ing a rat.' And he goes, 'All right, I've heard enough. Back of the van for you!' He didn't believe me, guv'nor. So I spent a few hours in the clink, didn't I? Finally I was able to call someone in production to come bail me out."

Far from angry, Rob threw an arm around Danny.

"Wow. I'm so sorry to hear that. We wouldn't have known what to do without you. I'm glad you made it out. Cary was getting kinda tired of wrestling a dummy."

The poor fellow seemed relieved.

"Thanks, guv'nor! It was quite an ordeal, I can tell you!"

"But you're okay now, right? Or do you need some time?" Rob asked.

"No, guv. I've been locked up all night. I'm ready to go."

And with that, there was a round of applause and a cheer from the crew. Within minutes Danny had transformed into a Rodent of Unusual Size, and helped us all find our way out of the Fire Swamp, once and for all.

✤ 6 ✤

STORMING THE CASTLE
AND BEING MOSTLY DEAD

BAKEWELL, DERBYSHIRE

After being given the weekend off to recover from our long shoot in the Fire Swamp the whole crew packed up and traveled to our next location: Derbyshire's famous Peak District, arriving on the first day of September. A good deal of the movie was to be filmed in and around this area, most notably at Haddon Hall, an ancient manor home located on the River Wye in Bakewell. I can attest that it's almost impossible to visit Haddon Hall and not feel a sense of awe.

In America sometimes it's easy to lose sight of the fact that the world is an ancient place. The United States is, after all, but a few hundred years old, a veritable blip on the timepiece of Western civilization. In parts of Europe, though, there is no mistaking the history; it is palpable and overwhelming. Haddon Hall has a very rich history. The place cannot be measured in years or even decades, but in centuries. You can feel the ghosts of medieval times; they practically whisper from the walls.

Parts of it date back to the late eleventh century, when the property belonged to a noble by the name of William Peverel the Elder, allegedly the illegitimate son of William the Conqueror, the great Norman king. It also has a wonderful romantic past, which made it a perfect setting for our tale. In the late sixteenth century, the property belonged to the Vernons, a powerful family closely associated with the infamous King Henry VIII. Sir George Vernon, known as the king of the Peak District, had a daughter by the name of Dorothy, who fell in love with a young local man named John Manners. Sir George, however, did not approve of the match between his daughter and the local fellow who was a nobleman (unlike our Buttercup and Westley) and tried to keep the lovers apart. According to lore, Dorothy's lover would arrange to meet her in the nearby woods for secret trysts, disguised as a forester so that he wouldn't attract attention. One night, in 1563, Manners spirited Dorothy away on his horse so that they could live happily ever after, much like the ending of our movie.

True love prevails!

Four years later, Haddon Hall passed into the hands of the Manners family, where it has remained ever since. The castle stayed intact for hundreds of years, until it was abandoned in the early 1700s and almost fell into ruin. In the 1920s, it was carefully restored by the Duke and Duchess of Rutland. Four years after that, Hollywood came calling, when a film of Dorothy's famed love affair, entitled *Dorothy Vernon of Haddon Hall*, and starring Mary Pickford, was the first movie shot there. More than sixty years would go by before the estate was featured in another film, and this time it was one I was intimately familiar with: *Lady Jane*. In fact, had I not been in that film, I don't know that I would have ever come across Rob's radar while he was casting. So there was, for me, a feeling of fate, or maybe serendipity, when it came to the place.

Needless to say I was thrilled to be back at the estate, which would double for Prince Humperdinck's castle in Florin. I knew it well and felt like I belonged there. And I'm glad to be part of a group of film-makers that helped alert the world to its exquisite architecture and the stunning beauty of the surrounding countryside. In the past twenty-five years, dozens of movies and television series have used the property for a period setting, including *Jane Eyre* (three different versions!), *Pride and Prejudice*, and *Elizabeth*. But perhaps no film has done more to boost the recognition of the hall and the tourism industry of the Peak District than *The Princess Bride*.

The very same sweet family, the Mannerses, who were living in Haddon Hall when I shot there only a year before were still living there when I returned, residing in one of the wings of the estate while the rest of the hall remained open to the public. I remember them coming out to greet us the morning we arrived from London. They were very gra-

CHRISTOPHER GUEST

I can only speak for myself, obviously, I've spent a lot of time in England and I like being there. So that was a good place to start anyway. But on the most basic level, the romance for actors of being in a situation where you get to dress up? This is what actors like to do. Putting on costumes of people from a long time ago and having swordfights, you know? It's almost like going to a movie camp where you just get to have fun. It was just one of those magical things. And even though I didn't know the other actors except for Billy, what subsequently happened was that it became a very tight-knit group of actors that were about to have one of the great experiences that you could have.

cious and friendly, and remembered me from *Lady Jane*, which was nice. Walking onto the property was like stepping back in time, not only to when I'd last been there but also several centuries.

It's one thing to film a movie on a soundstage, where you have easy access to the most current technology, without regard to weather or other issues that can wreak havoc with continuity and schedule. But working on location can be an utterly joyful experience, fueling creativity and an esprit de corps in ways that inevitably show up on the screen. I'm not suggesting that a gorgeous location can offset the problems inherent in a feeble script, unfortunate casting, or unsteady direction. But *The Princess Bride* was delightfully free of those weaknesses. We had the right actors, the right crew, the right script, and a sure hand at the helm in Rob.

Moreover, in Haddon Hall we had a setting that was ideally suited to our project. I can still see the looks on the faces of our art director, Richard Holland, and set decorator, Maggie Gray, the first time I saw them in the fourteenth-century banqueting hall that they had miraculously transformed into Humperdinck's study. They had the air and countenance of kids in a candy store. With its grand Tudor architecture and an abundance of medieval accoutrements, the place was almost like a movie set in itself. It provoked the right combination of epic scale and intimacy. Very little was required to make it look exactly as one envisioned it while reading the screenplay. That didn't prevent Richard, Maggie, and their crew from adding incredible designs to all the rooms we would be using, to give them that wonderful medieval fairy-tale flair.

"Pretty neat, huh?" Rob said as we walked around the sets.

"Amazing! Simply amazing."

I could tell from his demeanor that he couldn't wait to get started. He was genuinely excited. As we all were. I also recall, on our first day there, noticing a rather heavyset-looking guy with big red muttonchops and a pudding-bowl haircut, dressed in formal wear, following us around. It turns out he was the local fire marshal, or "fire warden" as they are known in the UK, assigned by the owners of the property to oversee our filming. They had been made aware by our production that there would be scenes involving fire and possibly open-flame torches on the walls, and they justifiably wanted to protect their very precious property from any potential damage. I remember this fellow had a look to him that seemed familiar but I just couldn't place it. It was Rob who finally made the connection.

"He looks exactly like Captain Kangaroo!" he said.

And he was right. So much so, that Sarandon and Guest took to humming or whistling the theme song of the show every time they passed him on the set. The poor guy had no idea what they were doing, since the *Captain Kangaroo* phenomenon never made it to British TV.

The next fortnight's shooting at Haddon would be focused on all the scenes that involved the exteriors of Florin Castle. The first scene up was one that takes place relatively late in the film, in which Inigo, Fezzik, and my character prepare to "storm the castle" to rescue Buttercup. Westley at this moment is still unconscious—described by Goldman as being "mostly dead." He is hoisted onto a perimeter wall outside the castle, with the help of his newfound allies, to assess the huge odds that face them before the assault. For this scene Norman Garwood and his team had designed and built a fake parapet on the outskirts of the property so that we could have a clear view of the Hall, now dressed with fake towers and sporting huge chevron-shaped flags to look like Humperdinck's fortress, in the distance.

I remember talking to Rob about being "mostly dead," and how exactly to play that state of semiconsciousness. I knew how to portray most things when it came to exploring a character, but being "mostly dead" was a new one for me. We discussed what coming back to life should look like, with only limited use of my body. The only description of this I had to go on was Miracle Max's line from the book, when he tells Inigo, "If we're lucky, the tongue will work and absolutely the brain, and he might be able to walk a little if you give a nudge to get him started."

I knew this was meant to be a funny scene, perhaps even a bit silly. But I also knew it had the potential to be ridiculous if played too broadly. Rob and I discussed the nuances at great length and I told him it might be interesting and kind of fun to see Westley not have complete control of his neck muscles after he came to; that way my head could flop all over the place at specific moments for comedic effect.

"Also," I said, "since Fezzik is so excited about Westley getting his motor skills back, maybe we could have him grab my head and use me as a marionette."

"I like it," Rob said. "Let's try it."

When André strolled onto the set that day, it was also the first time I had seen him in costume. Somehow it had the effect of making him appear even larger, if that was possible. Fezzik's uniform, as it were, consisted of a huge, thick burlap sack cinched at the waist, along with great baggy striped pants and massive leather boots. Since his hair was starting to thin, the hair department had provided him with a hairpiece that lent him a younger, more robust appearance. It was, however, extremely hot that day, unusually hot for that part of England in September, and by the time he arrived on set, André was noticeably uncomfortable. He experienced warmth and heat far more acutely than a normal person. And yet not so with the cold. As the production rolled deep into the fall, and the temperatures routinely fell into the forties, when most of us would stand around shivering between takes, wrapping ourselves in blankets and sweatshirts to keep warm, André, even on the chilliest days, either walked around in short sleeves or wore no shirt at all and had just a towel around his shoulder (which would look the size of a face cloth, given his magnitude). He was actually more comfortable in the cold. It was the heat that gave him trouble. Still, he soldiered on admirably. One of the makeup artists would occasionally mop the sweat from his forehead just before the cameras rolled, but other than that, he was always ready to go, with that beaming smile of his.

It had only been a month and a half or so since I last encountered him, but already I'd forgotten about just what an impressive physical being he was. André had that effect. Each time you saw him, it was like meeting him for the first time, in the sense that one could never really become accustomed to his extraordinary size. Memory did not do him justice. He had to be standing there in front of you, blocking the sun or enveloping your hand in his, like an adult taking the hand of a baby, before you really got a sense of what it meant to be in the presence of this impressive human being. Goldman said he was like the Pentagon— "no matter how big you're told it's going to be, when you get close, it's bigger." Each day when he walked on the set was like being reintroduced to one of the Seven Wonders of the World.

ANDY SCHEINMAN

André was a very sweet and friendly man, but he did frighten people sometimes. Robin Wright completely freaked out the first time she met him. She ran out of her dressing room in a panic. It was actually pretty funny. She didn't know who he was or what was going on. She just saw this giant man and ran away in a panic. I felt terrible for André, but he didn't seem to mind. He used to say that with children, "Half of them run away when they see me, half jump on my lap." Even the biggest, baddest dogs were afraid of him. Maybe they thought he was a bear or something. And that was just part of his life, part of his everyday experience, that people and animals—everyone and everything—reacted differently to him.

I can't stress strongly enough what an incredibly sweet and wonderful guy André was. Here was a man who had taken the cards that had been dealt him in life and instead of wallowing in self-pity, had made the most of every situation. He told me he suffered from a form of gigantism known as acromegaly, which I would find out later was a result of his anterior pituitary gland producing excessive growth hormones—which, in layman's terms, essentially means that his body growth was expanding at a rate twice to three times greater than normal from the moment he hit puberty.

Carrying his 500 pounds, combined with the acromegaly and decades of outrageous physical punishment absorbed in the ring, had left him by the mid-1980s in a state of acute pain, particularly in his back and neck. Yet André never complained. His outlook on life was relentlessly upbeat and his ability to put others at ease a thing of wonder.

ROBIN WRIGHT

He was a smiler and he never complained. You could tell he was in tremendous pain, but he would never complain about it. You could see it in his face when he would try to stand up from a seated position. But he was just the most gentle giant. So incredibly sweet.

Most actors who have experienced any degree of celebrity know the occasional discomfort that comes with being recognized in public. At least if you don't want to be recognized you could wear sunglasses or a hat.

But there was no hiding for André. When you are that big, there is no possible disguise; no way to shrink into the background. Even if he had not been the most famous professional wrestler in history, he still would have drawn a crowd of gawkers wherever he went. But it never seemed to bother him. Whether innate or acquired, he had an impressive ability to simply float above all the attention, smiling and shaking hands, even posing for pictures and signing autographs. He was a walking, talking handbook for how to be a gracious and grateful star. I think it's safe to say that he was easily the most popular person on the movie. Everyone just loved him.

MANDY PATINKIN
He was constantly being mobbed for autographs and pictures by people. And I remember one particular day watching him wait patiently while a hundred or so members of the crew brought their families to the set and stood in line like tourists at Disneyland to meet him. And he let every single one of them take a photo with him.

The only topic you could not get André to budge on was whether or not wrestling was fake or rehearsed in any way. I don't know if in André's case it was real, considering all the severe punishment he experienced, or whether he believed in the wrestler's code of never giving away trade secrets. I think, if truth be told, it was probably a combination of the two.

As the shoot continued I began to spend more and more time with him. And slowly he began to open up to me about his life. He told me he had two brothers and two sisters and that he was the middle child. That he grew up on a farm built by his father, Boris, in the small village of Molien, which was about forty miles from Paris. He told me that by the time he was twelve he had already grown to a height of six feet two and 240 pounds and that he was so big that he could no longer ride on the local bus that transported the other children to school.

Sometime after that, the great Irish playwright, Samuel Beckett, bought some land in Molien and decided to move there (there is still a street named after him). Being a handyman as well as a farmer, Roussimoff Sr. offered to help Beckett build his country cottage and eventually the two struck up a friendship. When the playwright learned of young André's issues with the school bus, he offered to drive the boy to school,

MANDY PATINKIN

I'll never forget, I was having lunch at the commissary at Shepperton with André, Rob, and Andy. And I was busy trying to connect with him because we had to be partners for the next four months, and I wanted to bond as quickly as possible. We were all chatting away, and at some point during the lunch I said, "So this wrestling thing, it's obviously all fake, right?" And the conversation just stopped on a dime. And André looked at me and said, "What do you mean?" And I went, "It's all planned, right? It's all fake?" And he said, "Nooooo, boss." And he was serious. André felt it wasn't a fixed game. That it wasn't decided who was going to win or lose. He was rather proud of that. He seemed very humble at that table, and very much wanting us to believe him, and to take him seriously. He wasn't playing games. I didn't feel I was being schmoozed by him. Ever.

explaining that he had a convertible—the only one in town—and thus, the only vehicle that could possibly accommodate André's size.

And so, for a time at least, the Nobel Prize–winning author of *Waiting for Godot* chauffeured the young man who would eventually become the most famous wrestler in history to and from school. I always said there might have been another play Beckett could have written, perhaps entitled *Waiting for André*. When I mentioned this to Billy Crystal, I saw a light bulb go off in his head. Later on he would make a very sweet film semibased on his experiences with André called *My Giant*.

I asked André what he and the famous author talked about when they were together.

"Mostly cricket," André recalled.

I can only imagine André playing cricket. He must've sent a ton of cricket balls into the stratosphere as a youth, hitting them with that powerful swing of his.

He told me he wasn't fond of school, where I'm sure he was teased by the other kids, and dropped out after only the eighth grade to begin working as a full-time laborer on his father's farm. He then took an apprenticeship in woodworking, followed by a stint in a factory that made engines for hay balers. I remember thinking André had to have been a proficient one-man hay baler himself. Bored with these prospects, he told me he left for Paris shortly thereafter to seek his fortune. He said he was first "discovered" by an entrepreneurial furniture mover who saw in the teenage André someone who could do the work of five men for the price of one. And that it was while he was shifting a couple of armoires at the same time into the back of the removal van one day that he caught the eye of a Parisian wrestling impresario.

"That's when I started to travel all over, boss."

It should come as no surprise that the moment André set his gargantuan foot in the ring at seventeen, he became an instant star. Within a couple of years he became both literally and figuratively the biggest (i.e., highest-paid) wrestler in the business, and a household name across the globe. He told me that after his first event fans began mobbing him. Especially in Japan, where it was apparently good luck to touch or "rub" a giant. They felt that if they touched him, they would get magic or some sort of power. And even though that made him a little uncomfortable, that didn't prevent him from going there anyway. He also told me that some of the top Japanese wrestlers were so scared to wrestle him they would suddenly "go on vacation" when they heard he was coming to town.

Once he started wrestling he basically never stopped since promoters would fight over one another to book him, given that his name on a bill guaranteed a sellout year in and year out. I asked him how many matches he had been in and he told me that he had been averaging about three hundred a year for the past twenty years. Which is pretty incredible. I subsequently found out from Andy that his matches with Hulk

Hogan had become legendary and that one of them, which took place at the Pontiac Silverdome in Detroit just before shooting started, even beat out the Rolling Stones for the all-time record for indoor attendance at a live event, with more than seventy-eight thousand screaming fans going absolutely ape at the sight of these titans. The wrestling equivalent of Beatlemania at Shea Stadium!

One day André pulled out a thick wallet from his canvas bag and motioned me over. As I sat down next to him he produced from it a handful of well-worn black-and-white photos. Some were of himself with celebrities like Muhammad Ali and others were of himself in his youth, looking very smooth, as I recall. I remember in one of them he was dressed in a very dapper dark suit walking down a street in London. In another he was lifting an Aston Martin off the ground with his bare hands—a talent he discovered while living in Paris. After that he said he used to move his friends' cars while they weren't around, wedging them in tiny spaces or moving them around to face the wrong way. I asked him if he ever worked out but he told me he had never been interested in lifting weights, which means when Fezzik says the line, "I don't even exercise!" it was a moment where art was imitating life.

I also remember there being a few of him in swimming trunks on the beaches of the South of France or in various studios in Paris either lifting numerous ladies on his shoulders or stretching his massive arms over their heads like a bird—another apparently favored publicity pose.

I told him he must have been quite popular with the girls.

"Oh, yes, boss," came the response, followed by that great, very deep laugh of his—precisely the kind you would expect from André, and which, over the course of the movie, we would all come to love.

Meanwhile, back on set: There were the three of us, Fezzik, Inigo, and Westley (Larry, Curly, and Moe in an alternate universe) ready to storm the castle. We rehearsed the scene a few times, making some adjustments to the timing of my head-flops, as per Rob's instructions. And, when we reached the point where he was happy with it, we began rolling.

However . . .

We got to the moment where I wake up from being "mostly dead" and say, "I'll beat you both apart! I'll take you both together!", Fezzik cups my mouth with his hand, and answers his own question to Inigo as to how long it might be before Miracle Max's pill begins to take effect by stating, "I guess not very long."

As soon as he delivered that line, there issued forth from André one of the most monumental farts any of us had ever heard. Now, I suppose you wouldn't expect a man of André's proportions to pass gas quietly or unobtrusively, but this particular one was truly epic, a veritable symphony of gastric distress that roared for more than several seconds and shook the very foundations of the wood and plaster set we were now grabbing on to out of sheer fear. It was long enough and loud enough that every member of the crew had time to stop what they were doing and take notice. All I can say is that it was a wind that could have held up in comparison to the one Slim Pickens emitted in the campfire scene in Mel Brooks's *Blazing Saddles*, widely acknowledged as the champion of all cinematic farts.

Except, of course, this one wasn't in the script.

At the moment of impact, I couldn't help but look up at André, at first wondering, like a good many others, if we were experiencing an earthquake and then, having discovered we were not, out of sheer concern for his well-being. The sonic resonance was so intense I even observed our soundman remove his headphones to protect his ears. As the fart continued, I looked back at André. What struck me, besides, of course, the sheer immensity of the wind, was that steam appeared to be rising from his hairpiece, which, given that it was a particularly hot day, was apparently not unusual for him.

It was, however, combined with the fart itself, a highly unusual sight. I remember looking up at him as a huge grin flashed across his face and remained there—a grin of both amusement and, I suspect, of blessed relief. Finally the roar subsided and the set fell completely silent. Everyone was in a state of complete shock, not knowing what to say or do, as is usually the case whenever anyone passes gas in public, especially in polite England. The next line was mine—"Why won't my arms move?"— but at that moment no words would move from my lips. They were in there somewhere, rattling around in my head, searching for an exit, but it soon became apparent that getting them to utter forth from my mouth was useless. Between the fart, André's grin, and the steaming hairpiece, I was done for. I could not help but burst out laughing.

Then André started to laugh, too.

Not a snicker, mind you, but that wonderful, deep guttural laugh of his. Then, as was usually the case on most movies when "the giggles" (as it is commonly known in our profession) happen, it spread like a virus, hitting Mandy, Rob, and the entire crew. Now it should be noted that when this happens on a set, some directors try to let the cameras continue rolling, in the hopes that everyone can regain their composure in a fairly short space of time and get back to the scene. On this occasion that hope was pure folly.

And so it went, for the next couple of takes, André's line followed by the sound of uncontrollable laughter. And not just from the three of us but from everyone as I tried to say my line, "Why won't my arms move?"

But it was no use. We tried a few more takes, but they were all in vain. Every time I would think I was past it, I'd look at André and his big grin and the smoking hairpiece, and the giggles would erupt all over again between myself, Mandy, and André. Finally Rob realized that someone had to try to get the scene back on track.

"Okay, guys, let's try this again," he said. "André, are you okay? You need to take a break?"

"No, boss. I'm okay." He paused. "Now."

More laughter, even from André.

"All right, I got an idea, guys," Rob said, nodding and smiling. "Just laugh it out. Think of the fart, and laugh until you've got nothing left. Until you're completely spent. Maybe that'll work."

We did and then we reset and started to shoot another take.

Concentrate, Cary! I said to myself before Rob yelled, "Action!"

But the more I tried not to think about the fart, the more impossible it became.

Then Mandy began laughing again . . . then André, too.

And so it went. We kept cracking up, ruining one take after another, until it reached the point where I couldn't even look at André without both of us losing it. Finally, I pleaded with Rob for assistance.

"You've got to help me on this. I don't know what to do," I said. "I can't get through the scene."

Rob threw an arm around my shoulder, and walked me along the parapet.

"It's all right, Cary. Just flip it."

At first I was confused as to what he was trying to get at.

"What do you mean?"

"Try to change the way you think of André. Think about what it's like for him, being a giant and getting laughed at just because he's different."

I looked over at André. He was still smiling happily. I looked back at Rob and knew he was right. The truth is, André may have seemed like one of the happiest and most content people I had ever met. But I'm sure there were times when he wasn't, especially when he was younger and trying to find his place in the world.

"Better?" Rob asked.

"Yeah, but now I feel awful," I replied.

"Don't. These things happen." He gave me a pat on the back. "C'mon, let's try it again."

Even though I still felt bad, the sage advice Rob had given me worked. On the very next take, we did it perfectly, and that is the take that is in the movie. After Rob yelled, "Cut," I immediately turned to André and apologized.

"It's okay," he replied, "my farts always make people laugh . . . That was a big one, wasn't it?"

He still managed to make me smile, in order to make me not feel bad. That's how special André was.

The following week we shot the actual storming of the castle with dozens of extras and a good deal of pyrotechnics, including Fezzik on fire in his holocaust cloak, with "Captain Kangaroo" hovering nervously off camera. We also shot nearly all the scenes involving Humperdinck, Rugen, and Buttercup, including her marriage and dream sequence, which brought out the better part of Bakewell's local population as extras. That was Bill's last week before heading to New York. This location also brought us the amazingly talented Peter Cook as the Impressive Clergyman with the speech impediment and the wonderful Malcolm Storry as the cowardly Yellin. In the courtyard we shot one of the final scenes of the movie, in which Fezzik shows up with the four white horses.

Meanwhile, during every free moment, Mandy and I were subjected to long hours of sword-training with Bob and Peter. I would finish a scene, and just as I was about to sit down, Peter would be at my side, blade in hand.

CHRIS SARANDON

Here's my favorite André story. I had two young daughters with me on location at the time. I told them, "Daddy's making a movie about a princess, and I'm going to play the Prince, and there's a pirate in it, and a giant." As soon as I said the word *giant*, my daughters immediately were like, "What?! Daddy, there's a giant in the movie? What's the giant like? Is he big? Is he really, really big—as big as a house? Is he as big as a car? Is he bigger than a doorway? Does he talk with a really low voice . . . or a high voice?" They were just awed from that moment onward. So I went to André and I said, "André, do you mind terribly doing me a favor? My children have talked about nothing but you. I would love to bring them over to meet you." And he said, "Of course," because he was so utterly charming and guileless. So I walked my kids over to André's huge trailer, which was the size of a boxcar. As we walked up the steps into the trailer, I saw André at the other end. And I said, "André, these are my daughters." And the moment André stood up, one of my daughters goes, "Aaaaaaaahhhhh!" and starts screaming in complete panic. Then her sister starts screaming. Now these two little girls are screaming at the top of their lungs and we finally had to leave because they wouldn't stop. So I go to see him afterward and I'm so embarrassed. I said, "André, please forgive me, I had no idea. They were so excited to see you, and yet when they saw you they were just terrified." And he just smiled and shrugged. "Don't worry. Either they come to me or they run from me." And that was André. He was very much at home with who he was. And the way people reacted to him was, either they flocked to him or they ran away in terror. And he was okay with it. There was a perfect equanimity about it. He was just the loveliest guy.

"Don't get too comfy," he'd say with a twinkle in his eye.

The training never stopped. Even on my days off I would rehearse with Bob at the Hallam Tower Hotel in Sheffield, where we were staying. When we left for Derbyshire, the set where we would be filming our duel was still under construction at Shepperton. It was understood that by the time we returned, near the end of the production, Mandy and I would be at least competent fencers, if not quite the legendary sword masters described in the script, and the set would be ready for us to practice on.

Since nearly all the cast and crew were housed in the same hotel, for much of the next few months we lived more or less as a family. From the hotel we would bus to various locations, including Lathkill, where we shot the Battle of Wits scene with Wally Shawn.

It's funny the way certain things fade from memory over the years, but other, seemingly inconsequential things remain embedded. Food, for example, was a source of endless discussion throughout the shoot. Being a New Yorker, Rob had been accustomed to working with American crews, but this was his first time working with an English one. I remember the look of disbelief on his face when he discovered that British crews were permitted two tea breaks each day: one in the morning and one in the afternoon; and while on location these included another sandwich break in the afternoon. Shooting would come to a complete halt while everyone had a cup of tea and a "sticky bun" or "chip buttie," which consisted of French fries covered in melted butter on a bun—a real treat for your arteries.

The first time a tea break happened Rob was bewildered. Even though he might have been warned about it in prep, it had obviously slipped his mind.

"What the heck is going on?" Rob asked one of the crew.

"Tea break, guv'nor," the crew member said. "Half an hour for tea."

Clearly dumbfounded, Rob responded, "You're kidding, right?"

"No, guv. Union rules."

By the time the crew returned from their tea break, Rob was fretting—or as close to fretting as I saw him during the entire shoot, except for the days when the weather got the better of us. He turned to Andy.

"Two tea breaks and a sandwich break every day?" he said under his breath. "At this rate we'll never get the movie done on time!"

David Barron, our unit production manager, who overheard this, let him know that this was not a negotiable issue. If the crew didn't get their tea breaks, we might be looking at a potential strike.

"And then," David said matter-of-factly, "we won't have to worry about the schedule, as we won't have a movie anymore."

There were other issues with catering. On our first day on location, our lunch consisted primarily of tiny meat-filled pastries, which they called chapati (pronounced "japuti"), supplied by an Indian caterer. If you Wikipedia "chapati," besides a video of how they are made, this is what you will find in the way of a description:

An unleavened flatbread (also known as roti) from Nepal, Bangladesh, India and Pakistan.

Now, I happen to be a fan of Indian food, having spent some time in that country, so the following story is by no means an indictment of that nation's extraordinary cuisine. But this story is about quantity, not quality. At first we were all quite surprised that we had landed a caterer that seemed to be exploring exotic fare to share with us all. We had illusions that our palettes would be sated by the myriad of flavors the Far East cuisine has to offer. Unfortunately that was not to be the case. The second day brought even more chapatis. As did the third. By the fourth day, the rolled pastries had become a running gag between Rob and Chris Guest.

Chris would come up with new, hilarious phrases every time lunchtime drew near, each one delivered with that deadpan look of his. I remember one of them being "Fancy a fruity Chapati?", delivered in a flawless Indian accent, which totally slayed me. Chris is always that quick with a ridiculously brilliant line.

By the end of the week, word spread that there were grumblings from both the mouths and the stomachs of our otherwise very patient and easygoing crew. Even André, being brought up on French culinary delights, took pity on all of us and his own palate. When fans ask me about André, for the most part what they know is about his wrestling and his legendary drinking. What most folks don't know about him is that André was actually a real connoisseur of fine food and even co-owned a French restaurant in Montreal. During a break in his shooting schedule on the movie he chartered a truck and took the ferry across the channel back to his homeland, ostensibly to see his folks. When he returned, though, he arrived back on the set with a crate of pâté, cheese, foie grois, and a crate of fine wine. The crew, who already loved him, worshipped him after that. David Barron tried to confiscate the wine, lest it have an "adverse effect on the shooting schedule" as he tactfully put it, but André assured him he would "look after it," which he did! So eventually Rob had to let the well-intentioned but highly unimaginative caterers go and asked David Barron to enlist the services of another company. Preferably a caterer that knew how to make more than one dish, I believe, was the polite request.

✦ 7 ✦

ROB'S TRAVELING CIRCUS

There is nothing ordinary about life on a movie set, particularly when you shoot a film on location for any length of time. There is a wonderful line in Cameron Crowe's movie *Almost Famous*, when Russell Hammond, the charismatic lead guitarist played by Billy Crudup, tries to explain to the wide-eyed, and increasingly skeptical, adolescent journalist William Miller, played by Patrick Fugit, the appeal of the endless nights living on the road.

"This is the circus," Hammond says. "Everybody's trying not to go home."

I've never been on tour with a band or with a circus for that matter, but I imagine it has something in common with the moviemaking experience. On most films you find yourself sequestered far from home with a tightly knit group of people, trying to create something special while passing the hours in ways most people can't even imagine.

When you are on location for months on end, your job almost becomes your whole life. You don't go home to the wife and kids at the end of the day. You have breakfast, lunch, and dinner with your coworkers, and in the evening you gather together over coffee or a drink and rehash the highs and lows of the day while getting to know one another. It can be an intense, almost claustrophobic environment. But with the right group of people, and the right director, it can also be the adventure of a lifetime.

And so it was with *The Princess Bride*.

Acting, by any reasonable standard, cannot be merely defined as just "work." Actors do get paid to work, but we also get paid to essentially play, something most people abandon when they enter the adult world (if not well before that). In a way, as I have said, there is something very childlike in getting to perform either onstage or on film. All kids like to play dress-up, whether it's cowboys and Indians or knights and princesses. When it gets to be both fun and work at the same time, it can be a truly wonderful, rewarding experience, as it was on this movie.

If I had to describe our production, I would say it was more like a circus troupe than any I had been on—traveling around Sheffield, pitch-

CHRISTOPHER GUEST

Everyone hopes, I think, when you're doing a movie that you get the cast you want and that everything is fine. That everything kind of goes smoothly. That people have fun and in the end the product is something that everyone likes. You can't really engineer that all the time, for many reasons. Sometimes it just comes together and, in this case, that's what happened. Maybe it's more boring to say this than to say that so-and-so was getting drunk and throwing stuff out the window. But it wouldn't be true. It was kind of a miraculous thing. I remember feeling that very same thing at the time. And I'm not just looking back and painting some rosy picture. It was approached in a very loving way.

ing tents, putting on costumes and makeup, and staging our show. If you think about it, we had a "show" that involved giants, little people, wizards, albinos, swordfights, and death-defying stunts (and plenty of clowning around), all with Rob as the ultimate ringmaster. Heck, we even had four white horses! Looking back I feel certain that Bill must've spent some quality time at the circus with his kids while the idea for the book was still fermenting in his head. When I asked him this, he just laughed.

I also think there is a reason everyone involved with *The Princess Bride* still enjoys talking about it more than twenty-five years later: it really was that much fun. There is a certain pride in the finished product, of course, and of being forever associated with such an enduringly popular movie. But it's the process itself that I remember most, and how much fun it was to go to work every day. I would say it was as close to a perfect moviemaking experience as I have ever had, or expect I'll ever have. That's a rare thing on a movie set, and it all starts with the director. He sets the tone for the whole show.

Directors, like anyone in the process of recruiting employees, tend to be on their best behavior when you meet them for the first time. They can be generous of spirit, warm, even compassionate. Unfortunately, one occasionally discovers from time to time (and in some cases not long after the ink on the contract is dry) that one has been tossed into

CAROL KANE
A director has so much power. If he were to be on the set, worried to death and always saying, "What are you doing now?!" and blah-blah-blah-blah . . . as an actor, you feel that. It tightens you up. Rob was quite the opposite. He was somebody trying to make a movie that would please him in a very specific, personal way. And that's what works. Not, Maybe they'll like it if I do this? He was tickling himself and that tickled the world.

a lifeboat with wounded people who have been using the medium of filmmaking to either exorcise their demons or air their dirty laundry or other hang-ups in public. When that happens it can be a thoroughly unpleasant and depressing prospect for everyone on the whole crew. One finds oneself asking, Oh boy, what have I signed on to?

Luckily for us, we had a director who, being an actor himself, not only nurtured his cast and respected their technical ability, but was the same with his crew. Rob was like a big kid on the set, laughing, applauding, encouraging, and generally acting like a fan as well as a filmmaker. Any guy who greets you with a "Hiya!" before saying your name is clearly someone in touch with their inner child, which is a beautiful thing. The unpleasant alternative is if you happen to arrive on the set to find out you are working with either a benevolent dictator or a narcissist to some degree. Then you find yourself in the awkward position of having to stroke their ego. But, every so often, if you are fortunate,

CHRIS SARANDON

We had such a good time making it. The set itself was, as you can imagine, a lot of laughs. It was such a collegial group. And we had a director who knew what he was doing, and who had a great sense of humor. As an actor, you know you're in good hands with Rob. So you never find yourself thinking, Oh, God, am I going to do this right? I've really been lucky in that I've worked with some great directors. And on one or two films I had experiences that I still tell stories about. Things like, just before you go on camera being told that your chin is, you know, that you've got wattles . . . or that you're not at all funny and you're not charming and you're this and that. And then it's "Okay—action!" Literally. But Rob is never like that.

you find yourself working with someone who is as excited as you are to make each day's discovery. Someone who views the entire process as an adventure, and invites everyone along for the ride. In other words, someone like Rob.

As I say, the director's mood and character set the tone on a production, and it has a domino effect. If the director is miserable, then invariably everyone else will be, too. If he doesn't know what he is doing and shows up completely unprepared, that's also a recipe for disaster. However, if the director is confident in his or her talent and is fun, cool, mellow, and so on, then you have "lucked out," so to speak. Fortunately for us, Rob is a relentlessly positive kind of guy. In all honesty, unexpected British crew tea breaks notwithstanding, I never saw him get frustrated. In fact, I never witnessed anything even approaching a temper tantrum.

CHRIS SARANDON
Rob is calm. After a take he'll say, "Oh, my God, you're such a craftsman. Thank you! But can we try it again?" Sometimes you could see him, just off camera, holding himself to keep from laughing. That's a great way to work.

He may not even remember this, but in fact only once during the entire production did I witness Rob briefly get his mettle tested, and even then it didn't last long. It happened when we hit a patch of bad weather while filming in the mountains of Higger Tor. Specifically the scene where the Man in Black confronts Buttercup about her "faithfulness." In the UK, exterior filming, or "shooting," as it is commonly known, can be a director's nightmare. The weather is, more often than not, completely unpredictable. One minute you can be experiencing a heat wave, the next a flood of biblical proportions. Sometimes you get all four seasons in one day. You can find yourself shooting a scene in which the characters are bathed in sunlight one moment, and then cloaked in shadow the next. And the way that clouds move in England, especially in the Peak District, can either be intensely fast or slow, to say the least. Both are a disaster for a director of photography trying to maintain continuity of lighting for a scene. Well, on this particular afternoon, we got two seasons: summer and fall. We started the day with glorious sunshine, which by lunch gave way to dark clouds, and steel-gray skies that would periodically brighten just long enough to give you hope, only to dash them moments later. This went on for hours, with the cast and crew sitting around waiting for a break in the weather.

Today, thanks to CGI and other technology, lighting continuity is not such a big issue. Computerized cloud cover is a wonderful tool for a director to have at his disposal. In those days, though, shooting outdoors in England you were always at the mercy of Mother Nature, no matter what time of year. So there we were . . . the whole crew forced to sit on the mountainside, waiting

ROB REINER

The weather is always an issue, especially when you're on a budget and you only have a certain amount of money to spend, and you want to be responsible. And the truth is you really don't have control over those things. You can get a little crazy. But you've got to take a Zen approach because . . . what can you do? You can't fix the weather. It is what it is.

and watching the clouds. And, as the day grew short, I could see for the very first time Rob's confidence beginning to wane.

Directors are by nature and necessity somewhat like generals. They are leading the troops into battle. And the enemy is time. You are constantly fighting it, trying to make it your slave, trying to control it. But on this day, control had been wrested from Rob. I remember seeing

Adrian Biddle, our director of photography, a truly wonderful guy just recently discovered by James Cameron, who had hired him for *Aliens*, patiently holding his small, tinted eyepiece up to the sky to gauge the speed of the clouds.

"How long this time, Adrian?" Rob asked.

"Could be fifteen . . . maybe twenty minutes," came the somber reply.

This was a long cloud cover. One that was moving at an extremely slow pace. The worst kind. We had shot most of the sequence in perfect sunshine, which is what we were hoping for in order to match that footage. This change in the climate was now cutting into precious time. Time we couldn't afford to spend just sitting around. I looked over at Rob sitting in his director's chair. His naturally upbeat demeanor had begun to wilt and he was actually betraying a little disappointment. I remember thinking it looked as if he had his own personal dark cloud hanging over his head, pouring a little rain—the kind you see in comic books or cartoons. I guess it's my nature but whenever I see someone down, my inclination is to try to cheer them up. So I walked over to where he was sitting.

"You okay?" I asked him.

"It's these bloody clouds," Rob answered, having taken to using British swear words. "But what're you gonna do?"

"Not much you can do," I said. "I'm sure we'll get through it, though."

Unfortunately, that didn't help. Rob politely mumbled, "Yeah, I guess," then slipped right back into his funk.

As I walked away, I noticed Andy stroll over to Rob. Then, without saying a word, he produced three Hacky Sacks from his pocket and then did the most amazing thing. He began juggling. Yes, you heard me . . . juggling. It was the most extraordinary and beautiful thing I had ever seen on a set or indeed anywhere, for that matter: a man trying his best to cheer up his friend—by juggling, of all things.

I can still see Rob sitting there, slumped in his chair, hands in his pockets, furry hood over his head, and that little, dark, rainy cloud hovering above him. And then something miraculous happened. A huge smile began to slowly spread across his face as he became entranced by the simple phenomenon of three bean-filled sacks flying in a circle. The little, dark cloud began to melt away.

"We good now?" Andy said, while continuing to juggle.

Rob merely nodded. And the next thing I heard was that laugh— that deep, booming laugh that carried across the peaks as they shared a joke. That was the type of friendship these guys had. You didn't have to push the right button often with Rob, but when circumstances dictated, Andy knew exactly which one to push.

I don't mean to convey a false impression that Rob is a guy who thought that every day was sunshine and rainbows. And I don't doubt that he endured some anxious, pressure-filled moments that I was not privy to. In fact, one of the true managerial genius-like qualities of a director is to shield his cast from those moments and to hide their own insecurities if they have any. In other words to keep some of their cards hidden, as Rob might put it, being a fan of poker metaphors. As a long-time thespian himself, Rob has a genuine affection for his fellow actors and, having grown up on sets, has a great deal of empathy for the film-making process. He is also very decisive, which is a very good thing in a director with a vision.

The only other thing that neither he nor Andy cared much for be-sides the weather in the UK was, as I have already said, the food. And, having grown up in England, I can tell you that traditional British fare has never been anything to write home about. Today TV chefs may have ushered in a new age of cuisine in the UK and indeed throughout the world. But to an outsider at that time, especially in the hinterlands of Great Britain, it must've seemed like a veritable culinary wasteland.

It's not so much that the food was bad; it was mostly just bland and unadventurous. So being decisive as he was, Rob opted to take the matter into his own hands and ordered a hibachi grill to be installed in his suite at the Hallam Tower Hotel. At the end of each day he would invite us all to gather in his suite for hamburgers and hot dogs. It was great fun, with Chris, Rob, and Mandy crooning harmonies to Rob's favorite doo-wop songs as he flipped burgers on the grill. Although these parties involved a beer or some wine they never went on too late, as we had early call times the next day.

ANDY SCHEINMAN
We were out there in a foreign world, making a movie. We were cut off from the real world, especially up in Sheffield. I remember walking in on the first day and asking the guy at the hotel, "What's the best restaurant in Sheffield?" And he says, "We don't have one."

One night, right after we had all gone to bed, the fire alarm went off in the hotel. Loud, noisy, high-pitched sirens. The kind you couldn't speak over, they were so deafening. Security personnel began to immediately clear the rooms, sending all of the hotel's occupants out into the street. We all stood there in the cold night air, in our pajamas, night-gowns, and robes, while the local firemen, who had just arrived, made sure that the building was safe before letting us return to our rooms. We all sort of milled around, occasionally making eye contact with one another, wondering which one of us was responsible for the mayhem. We figured it had to be someone from our crew, since we had basically taken over the entire hotel.

No one ever officially owned up to it, and I suppose it might have

CHRIS SARANDON

We were on location together for the first six or eight weeks, and we were all in the same hotel, which doesn't often happen. It was like being at a great summer camp. We ate together, if not in the hotel dining room, then in Rob's suite. We would sit around and eat, sing, and play games. It was just a great experience.

ROBIN WRIGHT

And so we would have these dinners four nights a week or whatever, in Rob's room. All of us together, because we didn't know anybody else and we were out in the middle of nowhere. And after a couple bottles of wine he, Chris Guest, and Mandy would always break into harmonizing old standards, and we would all join in.

been someone sneaking a cigarette in bed that triggered the alarm. But that seems unlikely, as it ended up happening two or three more times. For a long time I was convinced that Rob's hibachi may have been responsible and that he must've left it on by mistake. When I asked him later about it, he denied it with a smile and said he thought it was André, who also had a hibachi in his room, claiming that after eating the hotel out of all their food for that day, he was always still hungry in the middle of the night. Which is an image itself. Sadly, André is no longer around to defend himself, so I guess we'll never know who the culprit was.

Besides turning Rob into the crew cook, England had also somehow transformed him into a big darts fan. Not long after he arrived he bought a dartboard and had it set up in his suite at the Dorchester Hotel, where he and Andy eventually had to redecorate the wall from all the times they completely missed. He even brought it with him to Derbyshire. Strangest of all, he had also become a fan of sheepdog trials, which were on television almost as often as the darts competitions in Sheffield. He was amused that these two shows seemed to dominate the British TV schedule. I remember walking into his room one night, and there was Rob, transfixed by the trials.

"Cary, come here . . . check this out," he said, giddy as a schoolboy. "This has to be the craziest sport ever!"

"What is?" I asked. Rob then nodded to the TV. "Look . . . the idea is that each dog rounds up these eight or nine sheep and herds them into a little paddock, right?"

I nodded. "Yes."

"And each farmer that owns that dog in the competition uses his whistle to make the dog herd the sheep into the paddock, and the fastest dog to get them in there wins, right?"

"Right," I said, smiling at Rob's amusement. "So?"

"So . . . how dumb do these sheep have to be?" he exclaimed, gesturing at the TV. "I mean, after the twenty-sixth dog, they're still confused about where they should be herded?"

He was right. It was pretty funny. But that didn't stop him from watching the show start to finish.

❖ 8 ❖

TRUE WUV

I didn't know much about Robin before *The Princess Bride*. I wasn't even familiar with her work on *Santa Barbara*, so I didn't know what to expect when I met her. I'm sure she knew nothing about me, either. I was only marginally more experienced than she was, and certainly not as popular, as daytime fans tend to be fervently loyal.

I found myself thinking, Wow, she can act. She's funny. *And* she's beautiful. What's wrong with this girl? Well, truth be told, there wasn't a thing wrong. Even her British accent was flawless, which is not nearly as simple an achievement as you might think. I've spent a considerable amount of time in America, and listened to many Americans try to affect a British accent, and it's not easy. But Robin has a great ear, and, like myself, Billy, and Chris Guest, she loved to imitate accents. Not maliciously, but in a fun sort of way. And in doing so make a study of that dialect. I have always been that way as well. Whenever I hear an interesting accent, I feel an urge to make a study of it, too. Which I guess goes back to my father, who was an incredible mimic, and to my love for Peter Sellers, who may have been one of the greatest connoisseurs of dialects of all time. From his very first role playing an East End thug in *The Ladykillers* and all the varied roles in *Dr. Strangelove* to his flawless, yet wonderfully absurd, French accent portraying Inspector Clouseau in the Pink Panther series, he switched something on in my brain as a kid.

So naturally, when Robin and I arrived in Sheffield and heard that the folks from the Midlands had a very distinct vernacular, we would find ourselves trying to finesse the sound. As we were both Python and *Fawlty Towers* fans, we would watch their movies and shows on VHS whenever we had some downtime in our trailers. And it was during that time that I also turned Robin on to my favorite Python, Michael Palin, and one of his shows, called *Ripping Yarns*. In return she and Andy introduced me to *SCTV,* which I had never seen. Andy arranged for his office to have the whole series recorded, transferred from NTSC to PAL (the local format) and shipped to us on VHS on location.

Sheffield is also, incidentally, the birthplace of Palin. I am such a fan of his that when Rob asked me for suggestions of English comic actors to play the Impressive Clergyman, Palin was my first suggestion. It turned out that even though he loved the script, he sadly had to decline, as he was just about to play a character afflicted with one of the most notorious speech impediments ever put on film: Ken Pile in *A Fish Called Wanda.*

Rob then mentioned that Peter Cook had also been suggested for the role and asked me about him, as he was not familiar with his work. I told him we should get Peter right away before he changed his mind, as he was part of one of the most celebrated British comic duos when he partnered with Dudley Moore in the sixties. We were lucky to get Peter, as he was flawless in the role of the Clergyman with the flawed accent.

Looking back I think Robin's performance in *The Princess Bride* is vastly underrated. Her role was to play the victim—the titular Princess Bride—a young woman who goes through a lot of trauma, having lost her true love, but who has to essentially look beautiful in the process. Here is another description of her from the book:

> *Buttercup doesn't care much about clothes and she hates brushing her long hair, so she isn't as attractive as she might be; but she's still probably the most beautiful woman in the world.*

That was Robin's job: to look like a woman who would inspire a young farmhand to leave home and set off in search of wealth and security so that he might one day be worthy of her hand in marriage.

Sounds easy enough, right? Most people think if you're blessed with the right bone structure, or if you just let the makeup and lighting crew do their work, all you have to do is bat your eyes at the camera and your job is done with a role like that.

Not quite.

Buttercup falls in love, loses her love, gets kidnapped, is forced into an arranged marriage, reconnects with her one true love, and then lets him go in order to save his life. It really requires a great deal of emotional range. What it doesn't require—or at least doesn't display—is the comedic talent for which *The Princess Bride* is so well known. Goldman wrote a screenplay that we now know is filled with great, classic funny lines. Unfortunately, few, if any, of those lines are given to Buttercup. Robin is not merely the victim in the film; she is also the straight man (or, in this case, the straight woman). And even though Westley is not

CHRISTOPHER GUEST

Robin was very young. She must have been in her early twenties, but she was so astoundingly beautiful. And she was incredibly sweet. She did a wonderful accent, which is very hard for most Americans to do. And Cary was this handsome guy and had a great sense of humor. Fortunately the script is not just some straight part. It has all these twists and turns, and he has great lines. So it wasn't a one-dimensional sort of young hero part; it had a lot of other angles to it. It was much more nuanced than you would find in a conventional script. So here are these two people and they're surrounded by crazy people, basically. There are these two evil people, myself and Chris Sarandon, and Mandy is this out-of-control sort of guy who's out to get revenge, and there are some other oddities. But there's a spine of sorts, and Cary and Robin have to be kind of regular people. That's always much harder to do than to be the bad guy. It's just a dream to play the guy in the torture chamber because, well, it's a dream.

exactly a comedian, he does have some funny lines, and is involved in some rather broad physical comedy. Robin's character is permitted no such relief. From start to finish, she had to play it straight, exactly as the role demanded.

That kind of professionalism, I've since discovered, is more apt to be found in actors who have honed their craft on the stage or in television, as opposed to movies. This is especially true of daytime television. I remember one time when Robin and I were looking at the call sheet together after a day's shoot, and I couldn't believe the sheer volume of work we faced in the morning and the pages of dialogue we would have to learn. And Robin just shrugged.

To her it was no big deal. On *Santa Barbara* she had to routinely bite off vast chunks of dialogue with virtually no time to memorize or rehearse.

In fact, we were all kind of blown away by her steadfastness and professionalism; how she never dropped her character or her accent while the camera was rolling. Since her role is neither flashy nor funny, her performance is sometimes under-appreciated, which is a shame, because it's actually pitch-perfect. She never once overacted or reached for something that wasn't there. All of the action revolves around her character, and it was her job to capture that sense of innocence and helplessness—and she did it beautifully. Some actors frequently stumble through scenes and sometimes require a couple of takes to get it right. Not Robin. As I recall, she nailed just about every scene on the first take. She was flawless. The perfect choice to play Buttercup.

WALLACE SHAWN

I was impressed by how hard a worker she was. Not to be self-pitying about actors—I mean, obviously being in a movie is easier than being a coal miner—but she was incredibly hardworking and disciplined. And you know, she was clearly in a foreign country and surrounded by these fast-talking, very vivacious people, many of whom, in a way, shared an East coast, vaguely Jewish vocabulary that she didn't know. And she just did her job and was great.

I fell in love with Robin from the moment we met—as indeed did nearly everyone who either met her, or got to know her. She is a remarkable woman and a great talent to work with. All I recall is that we had a really fun time working together on the film. With myself as a pirate. And she as a fair maiden. Running off together in the spirit of love and adventure. I mean honestly, how much more fun can you have than that? I like to think that the chemistry between us translated onto the screen. I have already told you how much fun she is just to hang with. But she also brings that same sense of fun and joy to the set and can light up any room with her smile. She is so genuinely relaxed and comfortable in her own skin and also very focused at the same time. Getting to play her knight in shining armor on-screen also made me feel very protective of her off-screen—not that Robin couldn't handle herself in any situation.

ROBIN WRIGHT
I was absolutely smitten with Cary. So obviously that helped with our on-screen chemistry. And we also really enjoyed one another. We made each other laugh constantly. He was and is still hilariously funny.

In fact, I think it's safe to say that everyone felt protective of Robin. I know there is a famous story (that has now actually been made into a cartoon!) where Robin was really beginning to feel the cold chill on the Derbyshire moors while shooting her kidnapped scenes with Mandy, André, and Wally. And she began to get the shivers. And once you get the shivers, it's very hard to stop your teeth from chattering. So André, sweetheart of a man that he was, devised a technique to keep her warm that was very simple, really. He would use one of his hands as a hat on top of Robin's head. She said it was like having a giant hot water bottle up there. It certainly did the trick, and he didn't even mess up her hair that much!

In the years since we made the movie, the industry has acknowledged what those of us who knew her back then already realized: that she is an extraordinary actor. And she seems to only be getting better with time—something that can be said about very few actors. As I write this now, she is just a few weeks removed from her triumph at the Golden Globes, where she received the award for best performance by an actress in a leading role for her remarkable work as the devious and scheming Claire Underwood on the Netflix series *House of Cards*. In every role, she gives something of herself that's unique. She never holds back and has that rare ability to tap into something deeply profound within herself that is appropriate for the character. She is a very observant and intelligent woman. That is why she is a marvel to watch. And I am proud to call her a friend.

ROBIN WRIGHT
It doesn't matter how many years go by, I think there is a bond from that experience that will never fade.

Getting fried in the Fire Swamp. The pyro almost gave Bill Goldman a heart attack on the first day of shooting. H Stage, Shepperton. August 18, 1986.

Farming in burlap. Birchover, Derbyshire.

Swashbuckling in suede. H Stage.

Rodent control: Disguised as a R.O.U.S., stuntman and actor, Danny Blackner, attempts to bite my shoulder with rubber teeth during rehearsal.

Explaining that there are no "summer homes" in England to Rob and Robin. First day of the Fire Swamp.

Rob putting his wonderfully positive spin on the virtues of wrestling a foam rubber R.O.U.S. A somewhat skeptical Peter Diamond (far right) looks on with Ken Baker, first AD (second from the right), and my stunt double Andy Bradford (in the background). H Stage.

Experiencing André's mighty wind with Mandy.
Haddon Hall, Derbyshire. September 1.

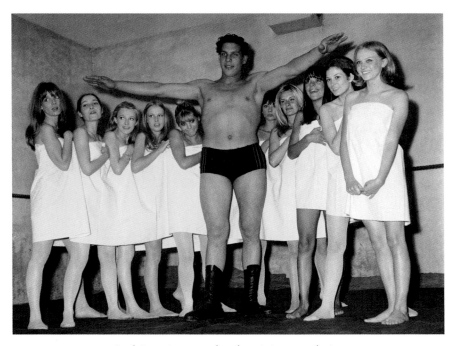

André at nineteen, already gaining popularity.
Paris, France. July 19, 1966. © *Corbis*

Chris Sarandon, Rob, and Chris Guest discuss week two of "chapatis." Haddon Hall.

Marveling at the sheer beauty of Buttercup.

Sharing a laugh with Robin. Cave Dale, Castleton.

In full "serf" gear. Watching Rob and Andy's new favorite sport—sheepherding! A scene that nearly made it into the film. Bradley Rocks, Birchover.

Attempting the Heimlich on André the Peak.
Stanton-in-Peak, Peak District, Derbyshire.

Another lost day to fine English weather.

BFFs Billy Crystal and Rob Reiner. Billy's outtakes for Miracle Max were so hysterical Rob and I had to watch them from a monitor outside the soundstage. "Miracle Max's Hovel," M Stage, Shepperton.

"We are but poor, lost circus performers . . ." Inconceivably, Wallace Shawn was so convinced that he was going to be replaced he gave himself hives. Hever Castle, Kent. October 22.

Defending Buttercup from . . .

these guys . . . Humperdinck and his stooge, Count Rugen. Within an hour of these stills being taken I would wind up in the hospital. Burnham Beeches, Buckinghamshire. October 31.

Not only am I not left-handed, I am not operating with a fully functional left toe, either. C Stage, Shepperton. November 11.

Mandy posing for his action figure. C Stage.

Chris wanted to have Rugen emit a fearful little fart just before running away from Montoya. Banquet Hall, Penshurst Place, Kent. November 26.

Rob instructing us in the nuances of The Kiss That Left All the Others Behind.

And captured! Six takes, all printed. D Stage, Shepperton. November 21.

My last day
of shooting.
From left: Andy
Scheinman, me,
Robin Wright,
André, Chris
Guest, and Rob
Reiner.

With Pope John Paul II and my mother.
The Vatican. June 7, 1988. © *Servizio Fotografico de "L'O.R."*

With President Clinton. The White House. March 5, 1998.

From left: Myself, Robin Wright, Mandy Patinkin, Chris Sarandon, Wally Shawn, Carol Kane, and Billy Crystal. Celebrating the 25th Anniversary at the New York Film Festival. Alice Tully Hall, Lincoln Center. October 2, 2012. *Photo by Stephen Lovekin/Getty Images*

Onstage at Lincoln Center. From left: Rob Reiner, Robin Wright, William Goldman, Wallace Shawn, Chris Sarandon, Mandy Patinkin, Carol Kane, me, Billy Crystal, and the moderator, Scott Foundas. October 2, 2012. © *David Godlis*

VIZZINI AND MIRACLE MAX

One of the great things about working on *The Princess Bride* was having an opportunity to perform alongside some of the smartest and most gifted comedic talents in the business. Just about everyone in the film had a chance to show off their comic chops, but I think two performances in particular are generally regarded as among the "funniest" in the movie.

The first is that of Wallace Shawn in the role of the Sicilian, Vizzini.

I knew Wally from *My Dinner with Andre*, directed by the great Louis Malle, in which he was both the costar and the screenwriter. The film contains some of my favorite lines, many of which are perhaps very revealing and personal from Wally's standpoint; for example, when he says:

That's what scares us. That moment of being face-to-face with another person. I mean, you wouldn't think it would be so frightening.

Wally, I should point out, is one of the nicest guys you'll ever meet. The kind of mild-mannered, amiable, polite guy who still uses words like *gosh* and *gee* as part of his speech. And he truly does have a "dizzying intellect," having graduated with a BA in history from Harvard and studied economics and philosophy at Oxford. Which is hardly surprising, since both his parents were journalists for *The New Yorker*—his father eventually becoming the editor of that magazine for thirty-five years and a very close friend of J. D. Salinger. After college Wally had originally intended to become a diplomat, but instead opted to travel to India as an English teacher on a Fulbright scholarship.

BILL GOLDMAN

I remember being at the casting session for Vizzini with Rob and about five or six other people. And the door opens and Wally Shawn walks in. He took one look at us all and said, "Oh my," and then turned around and walked right back out again. We had no idea what was going on. Finally he was persuaded to come back in and read and he was terrific.

While we were shooting at Shepperton, he and his longtime partner, Deborah Eisenberg—another brilliant writer, actor, and professor— invited Rob, Andy, and the whole cast over to the apartment they had rented near Sloane Square in London for drinks one evening. I recall being impressed by the remarkable library in the study and Wally telling me that it was one of the main reasons he picked the place. He also told me that during his time off he was going to give a lecture at Oxford on English and American literature, something that prominent universities around the world, not surprisingly, paid him handsomely to do.

Still, none of Wally's "dizzying intellect" as a writer, philosopher, or literature professor could dispel his insecurities as an actor. And even though I obviously do not possess anything close to his level of intelligence it was something I could easily relate to myself. I may be no dolt, but in a real "battle of wits," I am hardly a worthy match for Wallace Shawn. Frankly, I don't think many people are.

And the reason for his uncertainty? It wasn't a case of the first day heebie-jeebies that I had suffered but a real fear that he was going to be replaced. Apparently Wally had heard from somewhere that Rob had wanted another actor to play the role of Vizzini, and the rumors left him with something of an inferiority complex, as well as a near-crippling case of the jitters during production. I remember him being a veritable bundle of nerves from day one, starting with the table read all the way through to his final day of

WALLACE SHAWN

Cary is this good-hearted, lovely, fairy-tale character. And that's what the movie is supposed to be about in a way. So there was something always outrageously lovable about him during the filming itself, and to this day. He's just a genuinely good-hearted person and he was fantastically hardworking during the shoot.

WALLACE SHAWN

I knew I was wrong for the part because for whatever reason I had been informed by someone in my agency that it had first been offered to Danny DeVito and then to Richard Dreyfuss and that they had both turned down the part. The character, obviously, is Vizzini, and I know that Danny comes from an Italian background. I am from a Jewish background. But that was the least of my concerns. My greater concern was that I knew that Danny would understand the sense of humor that was called for by the script, and would have done such a beautiful job. And before every single shot of the film I imagined how Danny would've played it so much better than I could. I was haunted by that during every single shot of the film. So if any agents are reading this book, my advice to them is, don't tell your client that he's the third choice.

(continued on next page)

ROB REINER

Wally was funny. The first day he messed up a bunch of takes and kept thinking that I was going to fire him or something. I never thought about that. Never even considered it. But in his mind that's what I was going to do. He kept saying to me, "I don't really have a Sicilian accent." I said, "That's okay, Wally. This Sicilian talks just like you. He talks exactly like you." And he did exactly what I wanted him to do and he was great.

CHRIS GUEST

I remember a dinner I had with Wally in Sheffield, and he kept saying, "Chris, this just isn't going to work. Rob's going to send me home. This isn't going to be good." And I said, "No, no, it's fantastic! What are you talking about?"

ANDY SCHEINMAN

He kept saying to me, "I'm going to get fired, Andy! You're going to fire me!" And I'd say, "We're not going to fire you, Wally." I didn't realize it at the time, but he later said he had no understanding of the comedy of this movie. He wrote something once about the experience, and how miserable he was on a particular day, or in a particular scene. Wally is a highly respected playwright, but he was amazed that what he did in this movie is, in his own words, a thousand times more loved and respected as anything else he had done in his career. It's such a weird thing, because to this day, I don't think he quite gets why it's so good.

shooting. He told me later that every time Rob yelled, "Cut," after one of his takes, he felt for sure he was about to be fired.

I don't know whether his anxieties were based on fact or fiction. I do know that both Rob and Andy have said over the years that they never seriously pursued any other actors for the role and that they love his performance. Just as we all do. Rob told me he was not only an enormous fan of Wally's but even fought on his behalf to have him in the movie.

Rob also did everything in his power to calm Wally, and to coax what surely will be remembered as one of his most memorable performances. Much of the credit (and this is true of any of us fortunate to have been cast in *The Princess Bride*) should rightfully go to Goldman, who scripted the countless quotable lines, of which Vizzini was given more than his fair share. But Wally deserves recognition, too, for the unmistakable stamp he put on the character, and the unique manner in which he delivered those lines.

WALLACE SHAWN

To be honest, I didn't think Rob was very pleased with me. I mean, he never said anything like, "You're fantastic in this part! It's going to change your life! You're wonderful in the role." Nothing of that nature. I think he may well have been pleased by the time the whole movie was put together and edited, but I think that at least at first, he may have thought, Well, you know, he's okay but I wish Danny were here. Let me put it this way. I know that Billy Crystal and Carol Kane spoke about how Rob laughed so hysterically during their scenes that he had to leave the room. That didn't happen during my scenes.

A diminutive Jewish man from New York playing a tyrannical Sicilian crime boss?

Inconceivable, you say?

And yet, how perfectly it all worked. In hindsight one cannot envision anyone else in the role. But there were some interesting and tension-filled moments, when it seemed uncertain whether Wally would survive the production.

We began filming our only scene together, known affectionately as the Iocane Powder scene, or more appropriately as the Battle of Wits scene, in mid-September at a place called Lathkill Dale—a beautiful river valley in the Peak District.

Wally, bless him, was demonstrably nervous. Which actually helped me a bit since I was completely in awe of him at the time. Granted, I had seen only one of his movies, but that was enough for me. The minute he walked onto the set in his beautiful, ornate red and green velvet outfit, he looked like a wonderful prince from a Florentine fresco. Phyllis Dalton had even designed a matching hat for him—a flat medieval cap with a great big red feather sticking out of it. Wally tried it on once, quickly looked at all of our faces to gauge our reactions, and decided not to wear it. With apologies to Phyllis, it was probably a wise decision, as it might have been overkill.

As we began rehearsing the scene, I had no notion of Wally's insecurity, but I did notice he was sweating quite a lot, which struck me as odd because it was a rather chilly and overcast morning. Perhaps it was the heavy velvet doublet he was wearing, I thought. But as we continued to run the lines, his anxiety and perspiration became more apparent. At first I couldn't understand it. Here was this man, always the smartest in the room, experienced and lauded for his stage and screen work, concerned about a funny little scene in a fairy-tale movie. It didn't make sense. It wasn't until many years later when Wally would reveal what was in his head that day, that it all made sense. Even now I feel for Wally, because the schedule required him to film his most difficult scene (and without a doubt the most loquacious one in the entire movie) as his first moment in front of the camera.

If you've only seen *The Princess Bride* once or twice, or haven't seen it in many years, the Battle of Wits scene is the one with the long, complicated passages of dialogue between the Man in Black and Vizzini as they try to outwit each other and trick their opponent into drinking a glass of wine dosed with iocane powder, which is "odorless, tasteless, dissolves instantly in liquid, and is among the deadlier poisons known to man." (By the way, if you are wondering whether iocane really exists, it does not, except in the fertile imagination of Mr. William Goldman.) It might feel, in retrospect, as though Westley and Vizzini are burdened with equal amounts of tongue-twisting, mind-bending dialogue, but that actually is not the case. Not by a long shot.

Whereas Wally did all the heavy lifting in the scene, my job was fairly simple: to sit there and react to his character's histrionics. A subtle nod here, a slight wave of the hand there. One line of dialogue to every five or six lines spoken by Wally. In the scene, the Man in Black figures

ROBIN WRIGHT

Oh, he was nervous. He had a lot of lines to memorize. And Rob wanted him to recite it very fast. I think he was petrified of getting fired.

ROB REINER

It's true Wally had the most difficult sequence in the movie. The Battle of Wits was very difficult. But you know, I've heard from Wally, and from other people who've told me the same thing, that a day doesn't go by when somebody doesn't say to him, "Inconceivable!" Or ask him to say, "Inconceivable!"

WALLACE SHAWN

Here's another piece of advice that I'm going to give to any filmmaker who reads this book. It's not always kind to the actor to make his most difficult scene be the first scene that he does. That can be very, very hard. It takes a few days or a week to get into the mood of a picture and to get to feel comfortable with being in that film, and with the other actors, and to recognize their faces, etc. So to suddenly have to do your hardest scene on the very first day is not desirable. But obviously, scheduling a complex film sometimes means that's the only day that it could be shot. That's what happened to me. Actually, we shot it over two days and the ghost of Danny DeVito was devastatingly present the whole time.

that Vizzini is too clever by half, and that he will ultimately tie himself into knots trying to outwit his opponent. And that is precisely what happens.

Even though Wally was unconvinced of his talent in being able to pull off Vizzini, it's a beautifully crafted performance, and it anchors the most hilariously convoluted scene in the movie. It is both perfect and timeless. Even though it was stressful for him.

Equally stressful for Wally was his work on and around the infamous Cliffs of Insanity. The exterior shots of this sequence, where the Man in Black chases Buttercup's kidnappers up a cliff, were actually filmed on the massive Cliffs of Moher in Ireland, using stunt doubles filmed from a great distance to obscure the fact that it wasn't really me racing up the side of a sheer rock face and that André wasn't really carrying Wally, Robin, and Mandy as he hoisted himself up. The effect was achieved by using a massive crane and pulleys to yank the stuntmen up the side of the cliffs. It's kind of funny to look at the film now—the way it's so obviously not André pulling himself up, but rather Peter Diamond wearing a bulky suit and a rubber Fezzik mask strapped to a harness. And the speed at which the Man in Black scales the cliff. It really doesn't matter, though. In hindsight, it all somehow seems charming, much like the Rodents of Unusual Size.

WALLACE SHAWN

At my request, Rob acted out the part. Before I would do a section of it, I would ask him to do it for me. Then I would try to imitate what he had done. So you could say that what you see on-screen is a kind of collaboration. It's 40 percent me, 40 percent Rob Reiner, and 20 percent Danny DeVito. Because I was obviously in some way imagining what Danny might have done. And a lot of what I did was totally Rob's idea. For example, the way the scene ends where I sort of fall over sideways dead? I would never have done that. It was totally Rob's idea.

Our actual climbing sequences were filmed in comparative safety on the same soundstage at Shepperton where the duel would take place, with man-made cliffs that stood only thirty feet high. I wore a safety harness and was either reeled in effortlessly by a pulley or actually fastened to the plaster cliff for the dialogue, so it wasn't like I had to do any actual climbing. There were, however, obstacles to overcome for Wally's team. For one thing, André's bad back precluded him from actually "carrying" anyone or from being hoisted in a harness. So the crew devised a system in which André could stand on a platform attached to a forklift and hold on to Wally, while Robin and Mandy sat on modified bicycle seats next to them. All would appear perfectly safe and sound. Except for one thing:

Wally was terrified of heights.

While thirty feet of stucco and plaster might seem safe and surmountable when compared to the breathtaking 390-foot Cliffs of Moher, to Wally the prospect of scaling even a ten-foot wall seemed, well, inconceivable. I'm sure he didn't want to tell Rob too early in the production, in case he might provide the director with another excuse to replace him.

Once again, though, he overcame his fears and turned in an epic performance. In reality, it was also André's compassion and protective nature that helped calm Wally's acrophobia. In many ways André really was like Fezzik: a gentle giant.

Wally may have had some of the movie's most quotable lines, but if you were to stop people on the street and ask them to name a character in *The Princess Bride* besides Buttercup and Westley, I would be willing to bet that a great majority would respond first with "Miracle Max." This is surprising, given that Billy Crystal, who played Max, was on the set for all of about three days and appeared in just a single scene that

WALLACE SHAWN

I don't like heights and I remember at my audition I asked Rob and Andy, "Are we really going to be on the world's tallest cliffs, or what? We're not really going to have to do all of those things, are we? All those stunts?" And they said, "No, no. That'll all be done by stuntmen." Which was only partly true, because although we did not go to the world's tallest cliffs, we were obliged to act on a small forklift that in my memory couldn't have been more than four or five feet square, thirty-five feet up in the air on a soundstage at Shepperton. And even that was mind-bogglingly frightening to me. I would never have taken the part if I'd known we were going to have to do that!

MANDY PATINKIN

Wally was terrified of heights, and he was worried that he was going to ruin the whole scene. There was even a double for him on the set, just in case. But he stepped up to the plate, got on that forklift, and hung on to André for dear life. And André just patted him like a little kid and said, "Don't worry. I'll take care of you." I'll never forget it. The moment André said that to Wally, Wally calmed down and stopped feeling anxious. Then he just played the scene beautifully. And it was because of André's gentle assurances that Wally was able to even breathe!

WALLACE SHAWN

André was very kind that day. I was physically tied to him during the part of the film that was the most terrifying to me. He had a flask of cognac in his costume that he offered me. I declined because it was sort of dizzying up there anyway. And Rob was very kind also. He realized how panicked I was, so he shot the film in a way that minimized the need for me to be up there. So he actually gave up some very good shots out of kindness, which is a very unusual and remarkable thing for a director to do.

spanned less than five minutes on film. It is also perfectly understandable, given that this scene is one of the funniest in the movie. In fact, it is so funny and strange, and the tenor so unique, that it almost feels like it was dropped in from another screenplay. But it wasn't, of course.

Miracle Max is Bill Goldman's creation, albeit one supplemented by Billy's comedic talent.

We were two months into production by the time Billy and his on-screen wife, Carol Kane, arrived on the set on October 15. I had just finished another training session with Peter Diamond when I ran into Rob, who informed me that Billy had arrived.

"Can I go say hi?" I asked.

"Yeah, sure," Rob said. "He's in makeup."

For a moment I wondered if I would experience the unease that comes with meeting someone whose work you've long admired. As an actor, if you hang around Hollywood long enough, and if you are lucky, you may get a chance to meet some of your idols. Sometimes it's disappointing; sometimes it's exactly what you hope it will be.

> **BILLY CRYSTAL**
> I had this fantastic makeup, a character that was in my wheelhouse, and a director who totally trusted me and just let me go. I had the support of all of these people. It was just a little beauty. A perfectly constructed three-minute scene. You're in, you're out. It's really the definition of a good cameo.

Billy was every bit as funny and charming as I had imagined. He is an extremely down-to-earth person, yet seemingly incapable of not cracking jokes and generally just trying to make people smile. Some stand-up comics and some comic actors (Billy is both) are totally different people off-stage than they are onstage. Billy is the same person regardless of his surroundings. He's genuinely funny and genuinely nice all of the time.

As I entered the makeup department I found him sitting in a chair, patiently allowing his longtime makeup artist, Peter Montagna, to go about the painstaking task of transforming the thirty-nine-year-old actor into an ancient and cranky, troll-like wizard. We made small talk for a few minutes, with Billy grilling me about how the movie was going and saying how excited he was to be a part of it. Fascinated with his transformation, I asked him how he came up with the look for Max and I remember him telling me he wanted him to be a cross between Casey Stengel and his grandmother.

Then, as Peter began applying the last pieces of wrinkled latex to his face, Billy began reciting lines of dialogue from the script, searching for Max's character as he stared in the mirror. He even began improvising all these crazy impersonations of everyone who would end up influencing the role. It was absolutely hilarious. I felt like I was being treated to a private screening of a one-man show.

I realized at that moment that *The Princess Bride* was not only going to be a good movie, it had a shot at being a commercially successful one as well. I had initially thought it was such an unusual movie that it was impossible to gauge whether we had hit the mark, let alone whether there was an audience eager to see it. Billy changed all of that—or, at least, changed the way I felt about it.

He knew exactly what he was going to do with his character. Clearly,

BILLY CRYSTAL
I brought these two pictures to Peter Montagna, who was my makeup artist at *SNL*, and always did some of the great things that we did there, and continues to work with me. And I had the two pictures of Stengel and my grandmother. And we sort of just blended them together into the right look. I even brought in an uncle of mine who had a similar bone structure. He had long white hair, down to his shoulders, and Peter studied his face while he was making my cast. And I actually did a cast of my uncle's face at the same time. But there was all kinds of stuff that went into making Max look the way he did. Little things.

Mel Brooks was an inspiration. In fact, in the screenplay, his character is introduced as follows:

From inside the hovel a little man's voice is heard. If Mel Brooks's 2000-Year-Old Man was really old, he'd resemble this guy.

But Billy also wanted Max to be unique in his own right. I had heard there were issues with an earlier makeup test. That the prosthetics looked too comical, almost distracting. So he and Peter worked together for a while in LA before finally agreeing on the look. I watched as Peter applied each new set of prosthetics, occasionally taking a step back to let Billy assess the progress and practice some lines. He'd scrunch up his face, clear an imaginary wad of phlegm from his throat, and shout at his image in the mirror.

> ### CHRISTOPHER GUEST
> You had these two people, Billy and Carol, made up to look like they were two thousand years old, and there was definitely some giggling going on. I mean, that scene almost is a separate part of the movie. It has its own style.

"What!? What!? What?!"

I'll never know whether he was willing the character to life or perhaps just doing his grandmother. Maybe it was a little of both. Either way it was funny.

By the time Peter finally applied the last pieces of Billy's makeup, the wig and contact lenses, Billy had actually become Miracle Max. He was this other guy, this crotchety old man. Completely transformed. Hilarious. And once he was on the set in full makeup, he stayed in character.

I was also introduced to Carol Kane on that day. I was a huge fan of her work. Besides her performance in *Dog Day Afternoon*, I had also been in awe of her portrayal of Andy Kaufman's wife, Simka Dahblitz-Gravas, in *Taxi* and her roles in *Carnal Knowledge*, *Annie Hall*, and *The Last*

Detail. Here was an actress whose incredible body of work spanned more than a decade coming in to do a cameo in our movie. And while Billy's is the flashier role and the performance people seem to recall most vividly, Carol's work was also outstanding, and her transformation even more intense.

Today you can look at Miracle Max and you can see and hear Billy's voice. But Carol is virtually unrecognizable as Max's shrieking wife, Valerie. She is described in the script as "an ancient fury." And she was indeed ferocious in the role. But ancient? Hardly. People don't realize that she was only thirty-four at the time.

With each introduction of a new cast member, I felt more and more like a kid at theater camp who has been suddenly plucked from the ranks of the ordinary and tossed onto a Broadway stage.

BILLY CRYSTAL

I actually said to Rob, "Why don't you just cast Mel?" And he said, "Because I want you!" It was that simple, and I think in retrospect it was, for me, the right choice. But for the movie it probably was also. Because if you cast Mel, then suddenly it's, "Oops, there's Mel Brooks!" That would be a little too obvious and on the nose. I was not on the nose. I really was Max.

With Billy and Carol, the effect was intensified by two factors: the sheer amount of makeup and prosthetics, and the fact that they arrived so deep into the production and stayed for such a short amount of time. To be honest, I rarely saw either one of them when they weren't disguised as Miracle Max and Valerie. And it could not have been comfortable, slogging around for twelve, fourteen hours in thick makeup, wearing heavy burlap costumes, and toiling under hot lights. Norman Garwood had designed a magnificent little cabin in a fake forest to serve as their home. It looked perfect, but, man, was it hot in there once all the lights were switched on.

Not that Billy or Carol seemed even slightly distracted by any of that. Both of them brought their "A-game," so to speak, and in so doing created not only one of the most recog-

CAROL KANE

What I remember first off about Cary is that certain kind of nobility that he has. And that mixed in with an extremely impish sense of humor. Which is a very rare sort of combo. Because sometimes when a young man or young woman is that extraordinarily beautiful, they don't rely much on their sense of humor, but I think that when you crack the nut open, that's the delicious part inside of Cary.

nizable scenes in the movie but some of the most memorable days of filming.

All I recall from those three days of shooting at Miracle Max's cabin is that they were days filled with insane laughter. Rob said he wanted the scene to be outrageous, so he basically gave Billy free license to run with the character. Not that Billy needed much prodding. From the first shot in which cantankerous Max appears, poking his head through a wooden peephole in the door (very much like the doorman who greets Dorothy when she and her friends reach Oz), he began ad-libbing.

For three days straight and ten hours a day, Billy improvised thirteenth-century period jokes, never saying the same thing or the same line twice. Such was the hilarity of his ad-libbing that he actually caused Mandy to injure himself while fighting to suppress the need to laugh. Therefore you can only imagine what it did to me and to Rob, who had to leave the set because his boisterous laugh was ruining too many early takes.

BILLY CRYSTAL

The real joy was that the work itself was fantastic. The craziness of the movies—and it only happens in movies, or at Halloween—is that we go to lunch and there's Carol, all made up, and I'm with a giant, Mandy, the six-fingered guy, and we're all sitting down to have lunch together in the middle of the studio commissary. It was hilarious. It just was hilarious. I couldn't not be in character. Once you have the stuff on, you can't not be in character. So I'd order lunch in character as Max, and it was like, "How is the shepherd's pie? Is it spicy? Will I regret it in the morning?" And the waitress would be like, "No, sir, I think it's quite lovely." "Well, yeah, but you don't know my colon."

Some of the improvs made it into the film. For example, when Max opens the peep door, the original script called for him to say merely, "The king's stinking son fired me . . . ," in response to Inigo asking whether he is the same Miracle Max "who worked for the king all those years."

To better illustrate his character's bitterness toward the king, Billy decided to add the line "And thank you so much for bringing up such a painful subject. While you're at it, why don't you give me a nice paper cut and pour lemon juice on it?"

He also came up with the twisted notion of rating "true love" on a scale of the most important things in life with a sandwich.

BILLY CRYSTAL

We did some improvisation. I don't know exactly how much. It's so long ago. Rob totally let me go, but first of all, it was a very good scene to begin with. I think Rob wanted me to do it because I could bring flourishes. And it all worked really great.

"Sonny, true love is the greatest thing in the world . . . except for a nice MLT—mutton, lettuce, and tomato sandwich, where the mutton is nice and lean and the tomato is ripe."

André, dummy me, Billy, and Mandy

A quote that has since followed him in some form or variation into every deli and restaurant for the rest of his life.

Some of the funniest takes were just too blue, which is why they ended up on the cutting room floor. After all, *The Princess Bride* is a family-friendly PG film, meant to be appropriate and enjoyable for viewers of nearly all ages, so as you can imagine we really couldn't have

BILLY CRYSTAL

How could you not have fun? You've got a "mostly dead guy," a giant, and Mandy, and Carol. And a director who loved to laugh. The only problem with Rob is, he laughs. So sometimes he would ruin takes because he would laugh so hard that we'd have to say, "Go off the set! Go off the set!" He would just let me play around and find things, which happened that day: "mutton, lettuce, and tomato"—that's all stuff that just happened.

Max comparing true love to a vigorous bowel movement, funny though it was. Nor could you have him explain his foul mood by saying, "Don't rush me, sonny. I had a difficult night last night. I found my nephew with a sheep!" which couldn't have been used anyway since the entire crew, and especially Rob, lost it after he delivered the line.

In fact, these lines and countless others led to unusable takes ruined by us all giggling, and if you go to YouTube to find the outtakes, you can hear us all cracking up. For those of us who had never worked with him before, we realized that all Billy needs is a receptive audience and there is just no stopping him.

In some ways I had the most difficult task of all, as I had to present the illusion of someone who is supposed to be "mostly dead." Rob told me that I could not move at all. Not even a twitch. I wasn't even supposed to look like I was breathing, let alone laughing, as the camera would be able to see my chest moving. But the insanity of trying not to laugh while Billy was doing his ancient Yiddish stand-up would prove impossible even for me. I think he was actually trying to make me crack up during my one line in the scene when he pushes air out of my stomach, and guess what? He succeeded.

I just couldn't do it. After I had botched a number of takes, the decision was made to replace me on the table with the rubber dummy that André had been carrying around. I had to join Rob at a monitor set up in the hallway outside the soundstage where we had both now been banished by the sound department for laughing too much.

And it should also be noted that Carol truly enhanced the magic of all of her moments with her improvising as well. She created the whole bit with Billy regarding the chocolate-covered pill, bringing it to a level of hilarity that stands up to this day—offering helpful tips regarding ingestion and dosage:

MANDY PATINKIN
It was one of the most joyous times, certainly of my life. I can only speak for myself, but one wondered why we were getting paid and not paying them! The only injury I sustained in the film was off camera, when I was delivering lines to Billy Crystal in the Miracle Max scene. Cary was dead on the table, André was there, and I was off camera standing next to Rob, giving Billy his cue lines. And Rob couldn't take it; he was laughing on every take. He didn't want it on the sound track, so he had to leave the set after he called action. And I was stuck there, having to hold it together, while feeding Billy his lines. I literally bruised a rib from holding in my laughter. That's the only injury I got on the whole film. And, as I'm sure you well know, we did all the stunts ourselves.

VALERIE: "The chocolate coating makes it go down easier—but you have to wait fifteen minutes for full potency. And you shouldn't go in swimming after for at least . . . what?"

MAX: "An hour."

VALERIE: "Yeah."

MAX: "A good hour."

I have found that some of the most famous lines from the movie are quoted not only when people are thinking or talking about *The Princess Bride* but also when they find themselves in circumstances entirely at odds with the whimsical tone of the film.

My favorite story about this involves a man and his son whom I met while I was filming a movie in Rochester, New York. The father told me how the movie actually saved him from going insane.

I always have time for fans but this guy definitely piqued my interest. "How, if you don't mind my asking?"

He proceeded to explain that he had been on active duty in the

CAROL KANE
There are so many opportunities for anything to fall apart that hopefully you can take real joy in the process, because that's all you have. Anything else is just some extra added incredible bonus. What I took away with me was that this process was just twinkling in some way, that this group of people that I was in that room with, each and every one of them, were so extraordinary and so extraordinarily well cast that each day was delicious and valuable, and I was very grateful. I think that's the odd thing about the movie: we all felt that way.

military and had recently returned from a long deployment in Iraq. His base had been located in a highly dangerous area. There were lots of snipers, IEDs, and mortar fire, he told me. And after losing a lot of his comrades, morale among the unit had sunk to an all-time low. So every night from that point on, before the soldiers went out in their Humvees to secure the perimeter or go on patrol, their commanding officer would give them their orders and send them on their way with these words: "Have fun storming the castle!"

"Thanks to your movie we were all able to complete our mission on that base, as our CO was able to always make us smile before heading out. And that did a lot for morale."

I was very moved by his story. I guess you just never know how your work can affect people.

The only two actors from Rob's Traveling Circus the cast didn't get to spend a lot of time with were Peter Falk and Fred Savage. The scenes between Fred as the sickly grandson being read to by his grandfather, played by Peter, were shot just a few doors down on L stage, long after most of us had wrapped the movie. And, although I never got to work with them or even watch their scenes, I just want to acknowledge just how marvelous I think they both are in the movie. I was not aware of Fred's talent at the time but had, of course, caught many episodes of *Colombo* as a kid. Their moments together really anchor the whole movie and they are played with such loving tenderness that, for me they are some of the most moving ones in the film. Falk, incidentally enough, was concerned that he wasn't actually "old" enough to play the

CAROL KANE

I think my first day of shooting the makeup took something like nine hours. So I was sitting up in this chair and they were shooting already, and doing the parts of the scene that I'm not in. It was very frightening for me because they had all been working together for several hours before I was allowed out of the makeup chair. But then it just was so much fun and you know certain things were improvised, like the thing about the chocolate. But, of course, Billy is the master at that. The absolute master. It was almost impossible not to laugh.

part of the grandfather convincingly, being fifty-nine at the time. And he apparently arranged for the makeup department to put prosthetics on his face to make him look older. But after he saw the dailies, he turned to Rob and said he thought he looked like a "burn victim."

FRED SAVAGE

I remember Peter was in older makeup and he felt like it made him look too old. So we had to shoot it again with different makeup to make him look younger. He was so wonderful. No one was kinder and more patient, and made me feel more comfortable than Peter. Honestly, I don't even remember when we were shooting or when we weren't shooting. He would sit in that chair, and I would be in that bed, and he would talk to me all day. I grew very fond of him. Over the years he and I remained in contact. I had great affection for him. I was so devastated, as so many people were, when he passed away. That's what I remember more than anything: Peter and his warmth. I forgot all about acting or even shooting a movie. He just kind of became my grandfather.

✦ 10 ✦

A COUPLE OF MISHAPS

Filmmaking is not an inherently risky business, especially for those of us fortunate enough to be working in front of the camera. And, unless you are Tom Cruise, it is usually stuntmen and -women who handle the vast majority of tasks that could by any stretch of the imagination be considered dangerous. And even then, every precaution is taken to ensure the safety and health of everyone concerned. That's why there are safety meetings where the first AD and the stunt coordinator explain the stunts to the cast and crew and how to keep them and anyone else from getting injured.

That said, if you're young and reckless enough, you can probably find a way to get banged up in the course of filming a movie. Which is precisely what happened to me on the set of *The Princess Bride*.

Twice, in fact, although in the interest of full disclosure I should point out that only one of the injuries was incurred while I was actually working.

The first injury happened while I was simply behaving like someone whose sense of adventure exceeded his aptitude.

It happened in late September, while we were shooting the scene where the Man in Black taunts Buttercup about her true love for the Farm Boy, with the line "Life is pain, Highness. Anyone who says differently is selling something."

Another priceless Goldman gem.

Little did I know that I would experience true, agonizing "pain" only moments before I could deliver the line. Moreover, I would be the one trying to "sell something" different, just to cover my butt.

The spot that Rob chose to shoot this sequence was high up on a hilltop above a sheer ravine in a place called Cave Dale in Derbyshire. André happened to be there, as he was practicing with his stunt double, Terry Richards, for our fight scene later on. Early in the shoot it became apparent to the crew that it was going to be difficult to get André to any of these exterior sets since his size prevented him from fitting into the transpo van and his health precluded him from walking to and from the many steep, mountainous locations we were using. Therefore, production decided to rent him an all-terrain vehicle (somehow they found one big enough to accommodate him), and he just loved it. I'll never forget the image of André darting around on his ATV, laughing loudly—the already noisy machine groaning from the weight of him. It was a sight to behold. He could bring the whole crew to a standstill. What really made it compelling was that he clearly had a great command of the vehicle and knew what he was doing.

"I have one just like it on my farm at home," he explained to me one day. "It's fun, boss. You should try it sometime."

For reasons related to both the acknowledged rules of professional conduct and general self-preservation, I politely declined. Actors in the midst of a movie production are expected to refrain from activity that might in any way jeopardize their ability to perform in the film. This includes a broad range of activities, from the merely stupid to the outright dangerous. Generally speaking, these things would normally be written into a contract, which is understandable, really. If you are a movie studio investing millions of dollars in a movie, you have a right to expect that your star (again, unless you are Tom Cruise) will not go off bungee-jumping, skydiving, parasailing, rock climbing, dune-buggying, or ATV off-roading in the middle of the production. Even though there may have been a clause in my contract stating as much, common sense dictated that I exercise prudence and caution when it came to these things.

But André didn't give up.

"No, boss, really. It's easy. You'll like it."

I remember walking back from lunch to one of the transpo vans that would drive us all up the steep hill to begin shooting, and I noticed André sitting on his four-wheeler by the side of the road, chatting with Terry. As I neared the van, I heard that big booming voice call out to me.

"Hey, boss! Come here!"

I sensed what was coming next, but I walked over anyway.

"You want to try my toy? C'mon. You know you want to."

I don't know what came over me—what possible reason there might have been to throw caution and prudence to the wind—but suddenly I could hear these words escaping my lips.

"Sure, why not?"

Within a matter of seconds I was sitting astride the great vehicular beast, which seemed significantly larger and more powerful up close than it had from a safe distance. I should have known better, not only for the aforementioned reasons but also because I had no experience whatsoever on an ATV.

Terry, who was responsible for shepherding the vehicle when André wasn't using it, gave me a quick tutorial.

"Clutch is right here," he said. "Put your foot on it like this"—he pressed down with his own foot, then released the clutch. "Brakes are up here." He then squeezed the brakes on the handlebars. "It's just like a motorbike."

"Oh, okay. Cool," I said as he started up the engine. It was indeed loud. Louder when you are actually on it. A big grin came over André's face. He was happy to see me about to venture off on my first ATV ride. I had no helmet or protective vest. In fact, I was armed with nothing but hubris.

I released the clutch, and rather than easing slowly off the mark, the way it had when André had driven it, the ATV lurched forward, practically throwing me from the saddle. I held on for dear life, like a rodeo cowboy leaving the stall on a bucking bronco. It must've been a comical sight to the bewildered crew, watching me awkwardly try to master this four-wheeled bike. After a minute or so, I got my bearings and began to feel a bit more comfortable, so I foolishly decided to shift gears. As I applied the gas, the vehicle bounced over a thick patch of rocks, and my foot slipped from the clutch and became wedged between the pedal and one of the rocks, which caused the engine to sputter and stall. I looked down to see that the big toe on my left foot was bent straight downward.

If this sounds painful, believe me, it was. I let the pain wash over me in excruciating waves. I can still feel it to this day as I remember it.

It's an odd and no doubt particularly male reaction to feign indifference when confronted with injury in a public setting, especially when that injury is the by-product of one's own foolish behavior. I looked back to see Terry rushing toward me, along with several concerned members of the crew.

As they drew near, I held up a hand and tried to smile through the pain.

"I'm fine. It's all good . . ."

But I was merely trying to put on a brave front—kind of like the Black Knight in *Monty Python and the Holy Grail* proclaiming, "It's only a flesh wound!" after having his legs hacked off.

In reality, the throbbing in my foot was starting to build in intensity. But the initial pain and shock quickly gave way to sheer panic. This was a major shooting day for me. One where I would have to do a lot of walking around. Even running. Not to mention the daily fencing practice. How the heck was I going to fake that? I was so scared and nervous, not only that I'd probably get a serious talking-to from Rob for being so stupid and irresponsible but maybe I'd even be replaced. After all, how could I swordfight if I could barely even walk? So out of utter fear, I did the dumbest thing I could have done. I pleaded with those present not to say anything.

"I'll be fine," I said. "Don't worry."

They could clearly see that I was not. A medic was summoned, and, fortunately for me, like most medics, she was also a trained nurse. She carefully removed my black suede boot and sock, an enormously painful process in itself, and then tenderly studied my swollen big toe, which was pointing at an odd angle.

"Does that hurt?" she said, touching it gently.

"Mmm-hmm." I winced, clenching my teeth. "A little . . ."

Meanwhile my toe was sending my brain messages saying, Scratch that—a lot, dummy!

"Well, it's definitely broken," she said. "You should probably go to the hospital and get it X-rayed."

"Oh, no. I can't do that," I said, sounding more fearful than courageous. "Not right now. We have a scene to shoot. It'll be okay. We can do it after we wrap."

She looked at me as if I were crazy. *Maybe this guy hit his head as well?*

Fear had definitely clouded my judgment; I wasn't thinking rationally. I knew exactly what the shooting schedule entailed. I knew the way Rob liked to work. By now I had hit my stride with him, on most occasions printing my first takes and moving on to the next setup. I knew that we would be in this location only for this one day, and that if I were unable to shoot what we needed to get, we'd have to come back at a later date to complete it. Meaning, they would have to postpone my scenes and basically change the whole schedule while I got checked out and treated. I also knew that the doctors would most likely suggest that I shouldn't walk on it for a few days, perhaps even a few weeks, while my toe was put in a cast or a splint and allowed to heal properly. The whole thing would cost time and money, and that would all be on me. All these thoughts and more were running through my head at that moment.

I knew actors had been fired for less egregious lapses in wisdom. Even though he is not the freaking-out type, I envisioned Rob questioning whether I was worth the trouble I had caused. I'd be done. That would be it, I thought. They'd have to find another Westley. It would then hit the press and my career would be over. After all, who could blame them? It was all my fault. I was the cretin who didn't have the sense to stay off an ATV in the middle of production. Why waste any more time on me?

You see, it's one thing to get hurt while shooting a scene. If you get injured while filming, then everyone understands and feels bad for you. "Tough break, man. Don't sweat it. Go home and rest, and then come back when you're all better." Bond companies have insurance policies that cover these kinds of things so the producers don't have to worry.

But . . . if, on the other hand, you injure yourself fooling around *off* the set, that's a whole other kettle of fish. Sure, accidents happen. But this was an accident that totally could have been avoided. I had brought it on myself by messing around with a toy that, in hindsight, I realize wasn't really a toy. It is a dangerous machine. A machine I obviously did not know how to operate and had no business even trying to operate. There was a lot at stake here: jobs, money, insurance issues. It was a potential disaster.

Foolishly, rather than coming clean, I chose to hide it. In other words, I tried to get away with it.

"Please," I said to the medic and the genuinely concerned crew members standing around. "Don't tell Rob. I'm gonna be okay."

I remember Terry saying, "I think he's gonna find out, mate. I mean, your toe *is* broken!"

I turned to the medic. I was desperate at this point and starting to sweat profusely.

"Is there anything you can do?" I pleaded.

She gently cupped my foot in the palm of her hand.

"I suppose I could do a temporary splint."

"Really? Will it work?" I asked hopefully.

She explained that there isn't much else you can do for a busted toe. It was probably what the doctors would end up doing anyway, since toes are too small to put in a cast. She said they would most likely also recommend a lot of rest and ice. But, if movement is necessary, a small splint could possibly be utilized, even though not highly recommended.

"Do they have to do that at a hospital, or can you do it right here?" I asked, trying to mask the panic in my voice.

She nodded. "I think I can do it here. But it's still going to hurt. I mean, in other words, it's still going to feel like you have a broken toe," she said, trying to reason with an unreasonable person.

"Great," I said. "Can you please try?"

Naïve as I was at the time, I didn't realize that by asking her to do this for me, I was probably putting this poor woman's job on the line as well as all those present by asking them not to say anything. I didn't even realize that she would have to make out a medical report that would have to go to production anyway.

But I wasn't thinking properly. I was willing to try anything at this point. Like most Brits, I came from that stoic background of the whole "The show must go on!" thing. In other words, I was willing to do whatever was necessary to get the show back on the road. The medic opened her large first aid bag and began crafting a makeshift splint. Meanwhile, one of the ADs had shown up with a walkie-talkie to find out what all the fuss was about and, more important, to bring me to the set. I tried to enlist him not to say anything as well. As if that was going to work with a man with a walkie-talkie whose job I knew very well was to report any reason for delays to the first AD. I was so blinded by fear, I was involving all these poor people in my half-witted conspiracy to keep the very person who needed to know the truth from knowing it.

Now we had another issue. My foot wouldn't fit back in the boot! *Great!*

So we summoned a wardrobe assistant and asked for her help.

"I need a favor," I said. "Can you cut a hole in the back of the boot in such a way that it won't show on camera?"

By now an even larger crowd had begun to gather around. Had I been thinking properly, I would have known, obviously, that with this many people watching, word would eventually get back to Rob. But, like a soccer player trying to hide an injury, I was focused on only one thing: getting back onto the field.

I even began trying to fool myself that it was going to work. Here was my insane logic: With the splint anchoring my damaged toe and my sock covering the splint, it would be fine. The sock was also black; that way, if the camera were to pick up the hole in the boot, the glaring white bandage holding the splint in place wouldn't show up.

It might just work!

What a buffoon!

My toe, however, wasn't having any of it. It was still sending my brain more messages. Nagging things like, Really, dude? and Are you serious?

Eventually I was able to stuff my poor swollen mess of a foot into the modified boot. The maneuver itself was insanely painful. But, I had deluded myself that once it was on, and I was back on my feet, everything would be okay.

Clearly I figured wrong.

As soon as I tried to take a step, it was apparent that even through my toughest grit, I wasn't fooling anyone, least of all myself. I wasn't going to be able to walk without a limp, let alone run or fight a sword-fight.

I'll just have to fake my way through it, I thought. The AD helped me limp over to the transpo van and I was then driven up the long ravine to the set. It was perhaps the longest drive I have ever taken. Everyone in the van was silent. They were probably thinking, This deluded actor is out of his mind, poor sod!

As soon as we arrived, I put on the bravest face I could muster, hopped as best I could out of the van, and walked right over to Rob like nothing was wrong. Just eating the pain the whole way.

"Heya, Cary! How are you doing, buddy?" he said with a big smile.

I froze for a nanosecond.

Had someone already told him? Could this possibly be my last day on the movie? Oh, please, don't let it be so . . .

"Good. Thanks," I replied, praying that my face, which I was unaware was already sweating, didn't betray the strain.

"Everything okay? No problems? You're feeling good?"

"Yeah. Absolutely."

My brain received another "toe message": Hello? Anybody home?

He smiled in that way that only Rob could smile. It was a big, close-mouthed one.

"So . . . when were you going to tell me?"

"Tell you what?" I stammered, giving possibly the single worst performance of my career.

He just kept on smiling. I could tell he wasn't buying it. I think he even nodded a bit. The kind of nod that says, *Uh-huh.*

Finally, I couldn't keep up the pretense any longer.

"I am so sorry, Rob. I don't know what I was thinking."

He looked deep into my eyes and then spoke.

"Don't worry about it, Cary," he replied. "But you gotta know you can tell me these things, all right? We're all in this together."

He seemed hurt that I would try to lie to him. And he was right to. I felt like such a numbnut. I tried to explain the reason behind my secrecy. That I was embarrassed, but also worried that he'd be forced to shut down production. Or, perhaps worse . . .

"I thought you might actually let me go."

He seemed almost more hurt by that remark.

"Are you crazy? Why would I do that? You're perfect for this role."

"I dunno. I feel like a complete twit. Please forgive me."

"Don't sweat it." He then looked down at my hopelessly and obviously makeshift boot.

"Can you walk?"

"Yeah."

"Can you run?"

"I don't know. I haven't really tried yet. But I'll certainly give it my best shot."

"Okay, well, we'll just have to film around it if need be. Just don't be afraid to tell me anything. I'd be more upset if you didn't, okay?"

I nodded sheepishly. "Okay."

ROB REINER

I only found out Cary broke his toe because somebody had told me, "You're going to see Cary can't walk too good." He was limping around, obviously in pain, but it didn't bother his performance. I mean, he didn't have to do anything physical at that time, but if you look closely at the film, when he's on the top of the mountain with Robin, before she pushes him down the hill, they have this scene and he sits down, and he's leaning up against this log. And you can see the way he sits down, with his leg extended, he didn't want to put any weight on it. And when he did it, I thought, Wow! What an elegant way to sit down. I didn't realize that he just couldn't put any weight on his foot.

ANDY SCHEINMAN

It's so funny because now every time I see that scene, it's hysterical. Because all Cary is doing is basically trying to protect a broken toe. And the first time I saw it I just thought, What a cool move. You know? Those are the kinds of things you remember. When I watch it today, all I can think about is Cary having a sore toe, not anything about the scene.

He hugged me, and I felt his genuine love and support. What a mensch. I couldn't believe I had been so dumb as to try to hide it from him. But when you're young, sometimes you do dumb things. Like trying to show off your lack of skill on an all-terrain vehicle to a slightly bemused crew.

I learned a couple of valuable lessons that day, ones I've carried with me throughout my life and career. First of all, never try out a new sport on a film set unless the part calls for it and you are properly supervised. (I will certainly never set foot on an ATV again, that's for sure!) Second, always be open and honest, not only with your director but with everyone. The truth is always easier.

The fact is, not every director might have been as cool as Rob was about it. When we finished shooting for the day, we had another talk. One in which Rob made it clear that while he wasn't angry with me, he wanted to make sure that I understood the ramifications of my actions.

It was a fatherly pep talk about responsibility and prudence. I was in practically every scene of the movie, he explained. We still had extensive and complicated sword-fighting sequences to shoot. There was a lot riding on my health and viability.

Looking back, I think that was justifiably his biggest concern: that my foot wouldn't heal in time to film the duel. Don't forget, we had committed to staging it without doubles. In many cases you can work around an injured actor. But when it came time for Westley to square off against Inigo, it had to be just Mandy and me. And we both were expected to be at our best.

"I appreciate it, Rob," I said. "I'll be ready by then. I promise."

"Okay, good. Your health is always more important than a movie—always!" Rob said. "You should know that. But we need to know what's going on at all times."

The truth was somewhat murkier, however. I really had no idea whether my toe would heal in time or not. All I knew was that at that instant I was filled with enormous regret and embarrassment. And that my toe hurt really bad.

Immediately after wrap I was taken straight to the local hospital to get a proper X-ray done and a full examination, the results of which echoed the medic's preliminary assessment. I had indeed broken my left big toe, which had been bent completely downward when it was sandwiched between the clutch pedal and the rock. The doctor at the hospital removed the makeshift splint and applied a newer, smaller one. It would smart for a while, he said, but there wasn't much that could be done to accelerate the healing process. The best course of treatment was to stay off my feet. Here was a doctor telling a grown man dressed as Zorro to stay off his feet!

Oh, boy!

Best-case scenario was that even though it would still hurt, I might be able to at least move about relatively free of limping in approximately two to three weeks. I knew the schedule pretty well by this point. The swordfight wasn't scheduled until November, so I figured I had time to heal and get ready for the most physical part of the film. Up until that point, I'd just have to fake any scenes involving running or jumping. And rely on the magic of cinema to mask the severity of my injury.

But I'd be lying if I said I wasn't still completely racked with guilt and anxiety over the whole thing. We were six weeks into production. Deep but not so deep that I felt like I couldn't or wouldn't still be replaced, Rob's declaration to the contrary notwithstanding.

Over the next couple days we had to figure out how to execute the reveal scene between Westley and Buttercup, despite the fact that I was hobbled by a broken toe. Not quite *Misery*-style hobbled, thank goodness, but hobbled enough. In true Hollywood fashion, much of this was accomplished with smoke and mirrors, as they say. We shot our scene on top of the hill with the Man in Black taunting Buttercup about her love for Westley, then the sequence of them both rolling down the hill with Westley yelling, "As . . . you . . . wish," which I did in post. A shot that thankfully had always been planned with our stunt doubles, Andy and Sue. Robin and I then took our places at the bottom of the ravine, where Buttercup and Westley are reunited, apparently no worse for wear after careening several hundred meters down a steep hillside packed with rocks and other obstacles. It should be pointed out that by this point the Man in Black is no longer the Man in Black, as his mask has fallen off. He is once again Westley.

"Can you move?" asks Westley. An interesting question since I could barely move myself.

"Move? You're alive—if you want I can fly," replies Buttercup.

During this sequence, if you look closely, you can see that my leg is positioned oddly just prior to the moment when Westley crawls toward Buttercup. That's no accident. That is me trying to find a comfortable position for my poor, very swollen foot.

Moments later, Westley and Buttercup scramble to their feet and race toward the Fire Swamp, in the apparently suicidal hope of eluding Prince Humperdinck's soldiers.

Again if you look closely, you can clearly see that my character has a noticeable hop in his step. My apologies for that. I did the best I could to hide it, but a strange skip was all I could manage. Fortunately, since Robin and I were supposed to run together while holding hands, I convinced myself it looked appropriately awkward.

Fleeing, after all, is rarely a graceful exercise.

And neither is fencing, unfortunately, when you can barely walk. Nevertheless, I was allowed only a small reprieve from training. Peter and Bob came to see me the morning after my injury, asked how I was feeling, but expressed only a little bit of sympathy (which, to be honest, was about all I deserved). They then suggested we get back to training the very next day. Which we did. There was absolutely no messing around with these guys. They were concerned enough as it was about not having enough time to train Mandy and me adequately to meet the demands of the screenplay and the schedule. If we couldn't convincingly portray two men capable of staging an epic swordfight, then they would bear some of the responsibility. *Failure* was not a word in their vocabulary. Neither was *excuse*.

"Can you move your arms?" Bob asked me.

"Yes."

"Good, then you can train. Don't worry about your footwork," he said. "We'll just rehearse from the waist up. The arm movements are the key anyway. In the end, that's what the audience is going to be watching."

So for the next couple weeks, I trained while standing in place, going through the entire fight sequence without moving my feet, or by moving very slowly and carefully. It actually proved to be an effective method, almost like cross-training: by focusing only on the arm movements, I developed a deeper understanding of the sword choreography involved in the fight. I guess you could say it was an unplanned benefit.

A lesser injury occurred about a month later in Burnham Beeches forest in Buckinghamshire, not long after the pain in my foot had finally begun to subside a little. We were filming the scene in which Buttercup and Westley, having survived the Fire Swamp, find themselves exhausted, filthy, and ambushed by Humperdinck, Rugen, and a bunch of crossbow-toting Florinese soldiers. When it becomes apparent that there is no chance of escape, Buttercup barters for Westley's freedom by agreeing to return with Humperdinck and become his bride, an acquiescence that surprises both the Prince and Westley. Humperdinck agrees, albeit duplicitously, as he has no intention of following through on his end of the bargain. Before riding off with Buttercup, he says quietly to Count Rugen, "Once we're out of sight, take him back to Florin and throw him into the Pit of Despair."

As drawn by Goldman and played marvelously by Chris Guest, Rugen is a deliciously malevolent character, with an evil glint in his eye and an Inquisition-style zest for doling out pain and punishment. A menacing figure indeed, and the glee with which he accepts Humperdinck's orders is both humorous and hateful as he repeats the Prince's fake oath to Buttercup to return Westley to his ship, back to him.

"I swear it will be done!"

Moments after Humperdinck leaves with Buttercup, Westley notices the strange glove worn by Rugen.

"You have six fingers on your right hand," Westley says. "Someone was looking for you. He was . . ."

But before he can finish his sentence, Rugen cuts him off by hitting him over the head with the butt of his sword, knocking him unconscious.

I know I have said this about everyone in the cast, but it is true: Chris Guest is one of the nicest people you will ever meet. He is also one of the funniest. You only have to look at his body of work before and after *The Princess Bride* to know that. *This Is Spinal Tap, Waiting for Guffman, Best in Show, A Mighty Wind,* and *For Your Consideration,* to name but a few. For me, all I have to do is look at his face and I crack up. The man is a comic genius. Which only made his portrayal of Count Tyrone Rugen even more impressive. Of all the actors who performed in *The Princess Bride,* I would say Chris is the one who had the least in common with his character. Ironically, given that he is such a great comedian, Chris only has one funny line in the whole movie, when he says

CHRISTOPHER GUEST
Movie stunts involving contact with weapons or fists require a certain technical way of shooting them. Like when Mandy slashed his sword across my face in our duel, depending on the camera angle we could fake that because when we were shooting over my shoulder onto him, you could see the sword coming toward the camera. But when we shot the reverse, the sword was actually nowhere near my face, even though it looked like it was because of the specific angle. It's a trick, basically. It's like when people punch each other in movies where you technically have the actor turn away from the camera, which helps "sell" it. This was quite different, because there was no way to do that in this case. There was nowhere for Cary to actually turn given that the butt end of the sword was coming straight down on his head.

to Humperdinck, "Get some rest. If you haven't got your health, you haven't got anything."

For the most part Rugen is a sadist. Chris, however, wouldn't hurt a fly, gentle fellow that he is. So when it came to doing this particular stunt, he was concerned about even touching me with the sword. That's because his sword was a real sword. There was no rubber "double" on hand to use for the stunt. It was an actual metal weapon—dense and heavy. As a result, during the first couple of takes, it was obvious that Chris was holding back; I could barely feel the handle tapping my skull, which made it difficult to react appropriately. We tried it a few times, but our camera operator, Shaun O'Dell, told Rob that he could see that the sword was not touching my head and that I was reacting either too soon or too late. That's when I made a fatal error in judgment by opening my big mouth with a silly suggestion. One that I would come to regret.

"You know what, Chris," I said, "why don't you just go ahead and give me a slight tap on the head. Just hard enough that I'll get the feeling and then I think the timing will work."

Understandably, Chris was initially reluctant. As was Peter Diamond, who was on hand to coordinate the stunt. Eventually, though, it was decided after a couple of rehearsals that he could put a little force behind the blow, just enough to help me "sell" it. So we started to roll . . .

"Turnover!"

"Sound speed!"

"One forty. Take five!"—*Clap!* went the clapperboard.

"And . . . action!" yelled Rob.

Chris swung the heavy sword down toward my head. However, as fate would have it, it landed just a touch harder than either of us anticipated. And that, folks, was the last thing I remember from that day's shoot. In the script Bill's stage directions from the end of this scene state:

The screen goes black. In the darkness, frightening sounds.

Which is precisely what happened.

I woke up in the emergency room, still in costume, to the frightening sound of stitches being sewn into my skull. From the same doctor, no less, who had treated me only a few weeks earlier for my broken toe. I remember him saying to me after I came to, "Well, Zorro! You seem to be a little accident prone, don't you?"

And of course Chris felt absolutely terrible about the whole thing, even though I kept telling him it wasn't his fault. It was my dumb idea. But you know what? That particular take was the one that ended up in the film. So when you see Westley fall to the ground and pass out, that's not acting. That's an overzealous actor actually losing consciousness.

The next day on set, the cast and crew went out of their way to make sure I was okay. I'm not sure whether I was admired for suffering for my art, or looked upon as a bit of a nut, given that I actually asked another actor to hit me with a real medieval sword. I do know that I already felt like I had become part of a rather large and diverse family, if a bit of a clumsy, accident-prone addition.

On the 26th of October, 1986, we shot part of the sequence where the Man in Black climbs up the fake Cliffs of Insanity back on C Stage at Shepperton.

CHRISTOPHER GUEST
Cary was hurt. I cut his head, I believe, with the bottom of the sword. I'm not sure if it was a real sword or not. It might've been a real sword. But the handles were real, in any case, even if the blades weren't. Basically I just came down and actually hit him!

After we wrapped I headed to my dressing room and went about the process of changing from Westley back into Cary. I washed my face, dressed back into my regular clothes, packed up my script bag, and got ready to head home.

I usually like to listen to music when I unwind from a day's work. And, after Rob told me that Mark Knopfler had agreed to score the movie, I began listening to *Brothers in Arms* by Dire Straits, which had come out only the year before. I recall becoming hooked on the album all over again. And on the title track in particular. Rob told me that Knopfler had only one request before agreeing to do the film: that Rob had to find a way to place Marty DiBergi's USS *Coral Sea* baseball cap that he wore in *Spinal Tap* somewhere in the movie. Clearly Tom Petty and Sting weren't the only rock stars who had a special place in their hearts for the mockumentary. For those of you who never spotted it, the hat can be seen on a shelf in Fred Savage's bedroom.

According to the liner notes on the *Princess Bride* album, Knopfler stated that he "was only kidding about the hat." But Rob is the kind of guy who loves a challenge. Especially if it's a fun one.

Just as I was leaving my dressing room in my regular clothes after switching off the tape deck (this was the '80s, after all), one of the assistant directors came running up to me.

"Cary, sorry," he said out of breath. "They need you back on the set."

"Oh. I thought I was wrapped?"

"They need to get one more shot, and they need to do it quickly. Can you get dressed again?"

"Okay. But just let them know it's going to take a little while," I said, "as I'll need to put makeup on again."

The AD continued breathlessly. "Rob said not to worry about that. It's a wide shot so no one will notice. They just need you in your costume."

This sounded a bit strange, but not unusual. On a film it is rare but not out of the ordinary to be called back to set if the director suddenly realizes he needs another shot. Even after you have returned to your

ROB REINER

I had a good friend named Bobby Colomby, a record producer and a really cool guy who used to be the drummer for Blood, Sweat & Tears. So I told him, "I want to get a different take on this, you know? I want a traditional score but I also want it to have a modern feel to it, too." And it was he who suggested Mark Knopfler. I knew Mark had done the score for *Local Hero*, so I said, "Geez, that would be great because he has such a distinctive guitar sound." Mark said he would only do it if I put the cap I wore in *Spinal Tap* somewhere in the set. So if you look closely in the scenes where Peter Falk is reading the book, you'll see it in the background.

hotel sometimes. So I went into my dressing room, put my costume back on, grabbed my mask, sword, and gloves, and headed back with the AD to the soundstage.

As I walked onto the set, the first thing I noticed was a distinct lack of movement. Everyone was just milling about. They weren't working. They were just standing there . . . as if waiting for something to happen.

Then everyone turned to face me, revealing what they had actually been hiding—a large cake with *The Man in Black* crafted in icing and lit candles. They all smiled and yelled:

"SURPRISE!"

And then they sang "Happy Birthday" to me.

I swear I had forgotten that it was my birthday. I stood there silently, taking it all in. For a moment I thought I might cry, I was so moved as they sang. Instead I just laughed. I had just turned twenty-four and was in the final month of possibly the most important job of my career. I couldn't have felt happier or more at home.

✦ 11 ✦

THE GREATEST SWORDFIGHT
IN MODERN TIMES

I am often asked what my favorite scene is in the movie but it is difficult to pick just one, as that would mean weighing the importance of one scene against another, or declaring one moment in the film to be of greater significance or achievement than the rest. And the truth is I enjoyed the whole process. Certainly, from the very beginning of pre-production, it had been made clear to all of us—and to Mandy and me in particular—that the elegant swordfight between us would be among the highlights in the film. Moreover, that we were going to strive, at least, for something akin to movie legend.

And indeed there it was, written exactly that way in Goldman's screenplay: all capital letters, boldface type, and underlined twice, lest there be any doubt. Quite a thing to live up to. Whether we'd fall short of that goal was largely up to both of us, and the degree to which we

CHRISTOPHER GUEST

It took a lot of work for people who had never done that. And I had never done it, so it took a long time to prepare. We trained with these carbon fiber blades, because they're lighter. You don't use real metal swords because they're too heavy. And then they put in the sound later. In rehearsal with Mandy, I actually got stuck in the thigh; the point went right into my leg. And I thought, Oh, well this hurts. After that, I approached it where I was basically actually defending myself. It's a strange thing. We had our sword-fight in this eleventh-century castle, and it really was like a kid's dream, to be in a costume and having a swordfight in a place where they probably had a swordfight five hundred years ago. And I was making the sounds when we were fighting. The sounds that the swords would make, as you would when you were a kid—"Ch-ch!"—and Rob yelled, "Cut!" I said, "What? What's going on?" And he said, "Chris, we'll put the sounds in later." That got a huge laugh. The place just exploded, but it would be the perfect sort of thing a kid would do.

were willing to train and study under Bob and Peter. It should also be noted that Chris Guest had to train and rehearse as well, for Rugen's final encounter with Inigo. And even though that fight is much shorter and more one-sided, and perhaps the training less intense for Chris, it still meant double the training for Mandy.

Chris said that Mandy appeared really "pumped up" during rehearsal and that he had actually stuck him with his sword by mistake. After this accident, Chris apparently told Peter that he was going to throw out everything they had learned and was basically going to try to just defend himself once the cameras started rolling.

As for Mandy and me, through basic training and the first couple months of shooting, we felt reasonably confident about the progress we were making, despite my now injured toe. We had put in the time. That was never an issue—Bob and Peter made certain of that, filling every free second with practice. Our job was to put some meat on the bones of the fight, to create a duel whose physicality would match the brilliance of the words that accompanied it.

In mid-October, we got our first review while I was filming a scene with the great and greatly underrated Mel Smith. For those of you who don't recall, Mel played the gleeful Albino who preps Westley for his torture session in the Pit of Despair.

I'd be remiss if I didn't say a few words about Mel, who was another one of my favorite comedians growing up and has since, sadly, passed away. In the early to mid-1980s, Mel, his writing partner, Griff Rhys Jones, and Rowan Atkinson all starred together in a fantastically funny and popular British sketch comedy show called *Not the Nine O'clock News*.

Mel Smith, André jogging his memory, and Mandy

He was a wonderful improvisational actor and comedian, and, like Billy, clearly grasped the opportunity to embellish the small role and turn it into something memorable. Even though he didn't look anything like the character, it was a perfect bit of casting. With his white wig, bloodshot eyes, massive cold sore, and a delightfully fey manner seemingly at odds with the awful work he was about to perform, he truly embodied the Albino. And when I heard he would be joining the cast, I was thrilled.

"We got Mel Smith?" I remember saying to Rob. "You're kidding! That's great!"

I think Chris Guest, being the incredible connoisseur of comedy that he is, was the only other cast member who actually knew who Mel was. It took all day to film the Pit of Despair because, as with the scenes involving Billy, I found it challenging to maintain my composure. There's something inherently ridiculous about lying on your back, with suction cups attached to your nipples, staring up at Chris Guest and Mel Smith, pretending to endure searing pain while strapped to a massive "life-sucking machine." I remember both Rob and I lost it on the first take when Mel unexpectedly did that whole bit on the steps where he loses his balance. Then the whole coughing and hacking bit? Forget it. In the end I think I had to turn away during his off-camera dialogue just because I couldn't look at his face without laughing.

Since Inigo's character was not needed for the Pit of Despair scene, Mandy had spent much of the morning training with Bob and Peter between setups. At lunchtime we wandered over to the set for the Cliffs of Insanity where the swordfight would take place, so that we could give Rob and Andy a demonstration. After a few moments of stretching, and some last-minute notes from Bob and Peter, Mandy and I began the duel for the small crowd that had gathered, including some of the department heads and producers.

I thought it went rather well, and when we were finally done, Mandy and I, both covered with sweat, received a very gracious applause from everyone in attendance. I remember standing there with my sword at my side, my chest still heaving from the effort. Everyone seemed pleased, including Bob and Peter. Rob, however, had a look of not dissatisfaction, but certainly not one of complete approval, either. His expression was kind of blank. Scratching his beard, he walked over to us, deep in thought. He then looked up at us and asked:

CHRISTOPHER GUEST

What's unusual about this film is that so many people had great turns to do. You look at the richness of these parts and virtually everyone gets to do something that's memorable in the movie. That's very unusual and it speaks to the strength of the script and a way of approaching a movie where if all the parts are good and they're done well, it's going to be so much better than just having two stars and weaker supporting roles. That's a disaster, and it takes the whole thing down. And it happens a lot, unfortunately.

"That's it?"

I looked at Mandy. He looked at me. We both looked at Bob and Peter. There was a long beat, before I responded, "Yeah. That's it."

Not exactly the response we had anticipated, as I'm sure you would agree. Mandy and I had spent so many hours practicing and perfecting the duel, mapping out each and every step of the choreography, every thrust and parry of the fight, that we were now able to perform it not only fluidly but flawlessly without even thinking about it. We figured that was the goal. And it was—to a point. There was one thing we hadn't considered, though. By mastering the sequence, we had also shortened it. A duel that once lasted four to five minutes back in August had by now become considerably faster.

"How long was that?" Rob asked our script supervisor, Ceri Evans.

Ceri approached with a stopwatch.

"One minute, twenty-three seconds," she reported.

Rob shook his head solemnly.

"Not long enough. This is supposed to be the Greatest Swordfight in Modern Times—but it's over too quickly."

"What do we do?" I asked.

Rob shrugged. "Go back and add some more. Look at this beautiful set. We spent all this money. We built it for you guys. We can't be in here for just a minute."

Bob Anderson explained to him that we had pretty much used every part of the set and that if we added more we would be just going over the same terrain. Rob then turned to Norman Garwood, who was standing nearby.

"Norman, is there any way you could build up the ruins of a tower over there with some steps? Then maybe these guys could go up the steps, and play around up there. And then we could bring it all the way back down here on the level ground for the finish."

He paused. Norman nodded.

"Yeah, I think so," he said. Nothing was ever too much trouble for Norman.

"Great." Rob turned back to us. "You guys go back and make it longer and better. We need at least three minutes, okay?"

Bob, Peter, Mandy, and I all nodded like schoolkids who got a decent passing grade from our professor, but wanted the highest score possible. As a team we were shooting for 11 out of 10. Like Nigel Tufnel's amp.

At a subsequent meeting with Peter, Bob, and Mandy I threw out the suggestion that we collect every single swashbuckling movie available on video, including the ones we had already watched, and watch them again to find what we needed. Movies like *The Crimson Pirate, The Mark of Zorro, Captain Blood, The Black Pirate, Adventures of Don Juan, The Count of Monte*

Cristo, The Three Musketeers, The Scarlet Pimpernel, The Sea Hawk, The Prisoner of Zenda, Scaramouche, etc. And we did. We would fast-forward to the fight scenes and study them in detail to see if we could spot anything we could borrow or improve on.

We discovered that *Scaramouche,* starring Stewart Granger and Mel Ferrer, featured the longest, most intricate movie swordfight in cinema history. So our rallying cry became, "Let's beat *Scaramouche!*" Not the time, certainly (the movie's duel clocked in at six minutes, and we knew we couldn't beat that!), but we did want to at least try to beat it in terms of being memorable. In order to do that, we added all kinds of extra things—like going up the steps of the castle ruin, as Rob suggested, and almost pushing over a big rock—and then we agreed that we could add a bit of acrobatics, where we throw our swords in the ground, spin off a high bar, and dismount perfectly. Obviously that would involve the use of a stunt double, who turned out to be an accomplished gymnast named Jeff Davis. And since that particular stunt did not actually involve sword fighting, it seemed like fair game. Originally Jeff was going to do the same swing for Westley as he did for Inigo. I asked him if he could do a double for my character. Rob loved the idea and Jeff performed it immaculately on every take. We also added a piece where Mandy and I leap up onto some rocks with the use of a small trampoline and a somersault for Inigo as he leaps over my head. Also performed by Jeff. And a bit where Mandy would lose his sword for a moment, then catch it in midair.

I'm probably making this sound less stressful than it actually was. The fact is, the moment Rob said, "That's it?" I think I can speak for Mandy, too, when I say we became just a tad anxious. We had spent nearly three months choreographing one of the biggest scenes in the movie, and now, roughly a few weeks before we were due to shoot it, we had to go back to the drawing board and add two minutes or so.

Pretty scary stuff.

We'd been filming and training five days a week up to that point, but Bob and Peter now declared that Saturday would no longer be a day off.

"Sorry, boys," I remember Bob saying. "We have to get this right. And we have even less time to do it in."

So Mandy and I continued to practice and practice until we had carefully plotted out a sequence that would last approximately three minutes total, as per our director's instructions. It was a little harder for me, as my left foot was still tender, but eventually we felt we had it down cold. By the time Bob and Peter were finally happy with it, we were ready to put it on film.

WALLACE SHAWN

The swordfights took immense discipline and work, and they really did it. I have to say, I was impressed.

We began shooting the scene at 8:30 a.m. on Monday, November 10, on C Stage at Shepperton, which had now been marvelously transformed to look like a castle ruin at the top of the Cliffs of Insanity.

I had a lot of fun days while filming *The Princess Bride*, but this, for me, was possibly the most memorable. You could feel the magic on the set. There was a palpable sense of excitement and healthy tension.

While Mandy and I warmed up and reviewed the basic choreography with Bob and Peter, the set started getting packed with onlookers. Typically, only the personnel required for a given scene are allowed to watch. But now it seemed that everyone wanted to see us film the swordfight. I swear I saw the studio valet parking guy there, standing at the back with his arms folded, as if to say, *entertain me*. Even Bill Goldman flew back from New York to see it for himself—as if there weren't enough pressure.

I'll admit to having some butterflies in my stomach; they were mostly the good variety, though—the kind you get when you're excited, not when you think of failing. In fact, I think Mandy and I were so well prepared for this moment, we actually couldn't wait to get started.

Rob wanted to jump straight into the fight sequence itself and save the long conversation between Inigo and the Man in Black that precedes it—in which Inigo explains his obsession with hunting down the six-fingered man who killed his father—for later. We started with the simple lines: "You seem a decent fellow," Inigo says as the two men square off. "I hate to kill you."

"You seem a decent fellow," the Man in Black replies. "I hate to die."

If you look at it carefully, the choreography of the piece begins slowly at first, with the two masters testing each other, feeling each

ROB REINER

Cary and Mandy had to learn to fence both left-handed and right-handed, and we wanted to make sure that they could design a really cool fencing sequence. So when we finally got to it, I was so proud of the fact that the two of them—I mean, Mandy had started working on it even before we went over to London; he was working on it I think for about four months, and Cary worked for only about two months—I'm very proud of the fact that every single frame of actual sword fighting is both of them. There are no doubles except for the acrobatics when they flip off the bar. The actual swordplay, every single frame, is just the two of them. Left-handed and right-handed. I put it up against any swordfight in movie history.

other out. Gradually, though, the duel escalates in tempo, speed, and intensity.

"You are using Bonetti's defense against me," Inigo says, displaying both his knowledge of classic swordsmanship and an appreciation for his opponent. He already knows that this will be a chess match as well as a fight.

"I thought it fitting," Westley responds with a sly smile, "considering the rocky terrain."

The beauty of this swordfight, of course, is that it combines the execution of both physical mastery *and* brilliant dialogue. Goldman has Westley and Inigo exchange gracious, complimentary remarks about their opponent's tactics and style, even as they try to vanquish one another. In my humble opinion, it has never been equaled. Nor perhaps will it ever be.

"You are wonderful!" Inigo says at one point.

"Thank you," Westley politely replies. "I've worked hard to become so." (Never a truer line had been spoken!)

And then comes the beautiful moment when Inigo reveals that he is, in fact, not left-handed, and flips the sword into his stronger hand.

"You are amazing!" Westley acknowledges as Inigo pins him against a crumbling rock ledge.

"I ought to be after twenty years," Inigo replies.

"There is one thing I must tell you," Westley says.

"What is that?"

"I'm not left-handed, either."

With that, Westley frees himself, and causes Inigo to lose his sword. Inigo then uses a nearby (and conveniently placed) horizontal bar to perform an acrobatic escape maneuver. In pursuit, Westley does him one better: after throwing his sword expertly so it will stick in the ground,

BILLY CRYSTAL
The swordfight is fantastic. It's like a very beautiful, old-fashioned—in the best sense of the word—kind of scene.

he performs a double giant swing and perfect dismount, landing directly in front of the shocked but impressed Inigo.

"Who are you?" he says, legitimately curious.

"No one of consequence," the Man in Black responds.

"I must know," Inigo pleads.

"Get used to disappointment." One of my favorite Goldman lines.

Mandy then gave the most wonderful unscripted response to this line, a kind of mumbled "Okay" with a little shrug, much like a Spaniard would do, before returning to the duel.

The fight continues, until Westley knocks Inigo's sword from his hand and holds his blade against the Spaniard's throat.

"Kill me quickly," Inigo demands proudly.

But Westley has other plans. "I would as soon destroy a stained-glass window as an artist like yourself; however, since I can't have you following me, either . . ."

And with that, Westley uses the butt of his sword to knock Inigo unconscious. After my mishap with Chris, it was decided this time that I should walk behind Mandy and swipe the back of his head without actually touching him. An easy "sell" for the camera, and no one would have to go to the hospital. "It's only a mistake if you don't learn from it," as my father used to say.

We did the entire fight sequence from start to finish with Mandy and me (sans the acrobatics, of course) in a single take. Rob captured it on two cameras, from different angles, and I am proud to say, we did not make a single mistake. When we finished, the entire crowd in attendance burst into applause. Bob and Peter were beaming, Goldman was speechless. Only my big toe remained unimpressed.

"Great job, guys!" Rob said. "Fantastic! Now let's do it again."

And so we did.

Over and over and over.

One day became two. Two days became three. Three then became four. In all we ended up spending the better part of a week filming the Greatest Swordfight in Modern Times, which I suppose is appropriate. We shot from the front, from the back, wide angles, close-ups, from my point of view, Mandy's point of view, etc. At one point we even shot seventeen takes from a single angle. All printed. After the tenth take, I remember Rob saying, "Verr-y cool!" in that voice of his.

And then we did seven more.

I remember feeling a true kinship with Mandy that week. The truth is, while we certainly got along very well throughout the production, we really didn't get to spend a lot of time socializing on the set, as we spent most if not all of our spare time training. By the time we were done with that, and after a long day of shooting, all we wanted to do was go home and soak our weary limbs in a hot bath. During the shooting of the actual fight, however, I remember feeling very close to him. Probably in much the same way that boxers might grow close to each other despite being opponents. We would sit there together between takes, trying to stay hydrated, wiping our faces and hands with towels, talking about what we had done right and wrong, what had worked and what hadn't worked. Generally helping each other out. We'd go over the things we

MANDY PATINKIN

Rob wanted the actors to be seen doing all the fencing. He wanted full-body shots, as opposed to most other fencing pictures, where it would be the point of view of the actors. Where you would see only the hand of the other fencer off camera. In most movies, this would be done by a stunt double. But Rob was adamant that we do all the fighting ourselves. My greatest memory and pleasure, in terms of fencing, was the fact that we became proficient enough to improvise on a dime. I remember on one of the final days of shooting the sequence where we were going up the stairs, changing from the left to the right hand, it didn't quite work for the camera. And I remember turning to Bob Anderson, a beautiful man, God rest his soul, and he had a suggestion. I said, "Go tell Rob." And he said, "Oh, no, that's not my place." I said, "Bob, he doesn't know anything about fencing. You're the guy! You've got to tell him." So Cary and I went over with Bob and Peter and we told him. And Rob took a moment and then said, "Okay, go ahead and fix it. But make it quick!" We only had about twenty minutes, and we rechoreographed that whole sequence, which we had spent weeks choreographing within an inch of its life. We had learned the skill, the basics of fencing, so clearly that Cary and I, with Bob and Peter's expert guidance, were able to redo the whole sequence up the steps in less than a half hour. That was the highlight of the whole film for me, because we had really learned a skill and we were able to implement it instantly. That was quite thrilling.

had been taught: holding the blade correctly, bending our knees, staying limber and loose, and so on. And, most important of all, making sure we were always looking at each other's eyes.

If you look closely at the fight scene, you'll notice that Mandy and I are staring at each other throughout, telegraphing the next move or parry, actually kind of signaling to one another. We had it down to a very precise routine. So much so that the eye triggers basically became supplemental. There was no margin for error. Bob and Peter kept warning us that if we screwed up, it wasn't so much that the scene would be ruined, your partner might get hurt.

But to our credit we came out cleanly, without so much as a bump or a scratch. And with exactly the scene Rob wanted to capture on film, clocking in at approximately three minutes and ten seconds. A scene that I think did justice to the way it was described on the printed page: *The Greatest Swordfight in Modern Times.*

MANDY PATINKIN
At one point Rob said, "I want to put the cameras all the way up to the ceiling and do a couple more takes. Are you guys up to it?" This was after we had spent several days doing these fights, and we just jumped at it like wild animals. We did the whole piece without stopping again, like a stage piece. And the only painful moments to me were every time Rob yelled, "Cut! Print!" Because that meant we got it right, and we might not be doing that part again. That was heartbreaking to me. I just didn't want it to end.

❖ 12 ❖

ALL GOOD THINGS . . .

Iｔ's true in life, as in the movies, that the greatest highs are often followed by the lowest lows. The day after we finished shooting the
sword-fighting scene, I took a day to visit my ailing grandfather in
the hospital. He had been diagnosed with diabetes, but it was only after
I arrived that I was told that he had taken a turn for the worse.

Some people barely get to know their grandparents. People take
jobs in far-off places, families become fragmented, and generations occasionally lose track of each other. It happens. But I was one of those
fortunate kids who grew up in close proximity to their grandparents,
and I developed an especially close relationship with my grandfather.
His name was Billy McLean, and he was a true adventurer if ever there
was one.

I don't mean he seemed "adventurous" to a little boy (although he certainly was that as well). This man was the real deal. He had worked in military intelligence for the British government, and had been sent on undercover missions to all kinds of exotic and dangerous places both during and after World War II. He had even met Ian Fleming, who had been in naval intelligence and who had subsequently used his experiences in that field to create the James Bond character. When he first joined the army, Billy became part of the Royal Scots Greys (originally a Scottish cavalry regiment). So he had all these wonderful ancient regimental swords that he kept on a table in his study. They were just beautiful and they were also my introduction to the almost incongruous elegance of swords. When I was old enough he used to let me handle them and I imagined myself, among other things, as a swashbuckling pirate.

I adored spending time with him, listening to him recount epic tales of his adventures in far-off places, much like Errol Flynn's character does with the little Indian boy in the film version of Rudyard Kipling's *Kim*. As he shared these stories with so much love, it also reminded me of the way Peter Falk's Grandfather shares his love of adventure with Fred Savage's character in our movie. Which is why those scenes so resonated with me when I first read the book. Let's be honest: for a kid, is there anything better than having a grandfather who not only fought for his country but was actually a secret agent? I don't doubt that my grandfather suffered from some of the effects of his combat service, but he never once let on. Instead, he shared with me a passion for adventure and for life itself.

He was the real hero in my world and I treasured him.

And he loved me. Loved spending time with me. When he found out that I had gotten the part of Westley in *The Princess Bride*, he was thrilled. He knew about the book, that it was an adventure story and that I'd be playing a dashing pirate. He was proud of my success, and he had been really looking forward to visiting the set to see me at work. Particularly seeing the famous duel itself.

Unfortunately, he never got the chance, as he fell ill around that time. When I went to visit him in the hospital he was only semilucid. Age and the medication the doctors had given him had sapped his strength. Nevertheless, as I sat by his side and held his hand, I told him all about the shoot and how fun it had been. About André the Giant. About the swordfight, and how much he would enjoy watching it on the big screen one day. I even shared with him how much of a clot I had been, breaking my toe on the all-terrain vehicle. And then it dawned on me. It seemed as if the roles had been reversed. Here I was, the grandson recounting tales of adventure to the grandfather. At the end of it, I kissed him tenderly on the cheek. Then, unable to fight back the tears, I told him how much I loved him. I realized I was actually having my "As You Wish" moment with him.

It appeared that he understood what I was saying. I'd like to think so, anyway. Sadly, he passed away in the early hours of the following morning, surrounded by his close friends and family.

The next day I shared the news with Rob and some of the cast and crew when I arrived on the set. And pretty soon everyone knew about my loss. They couldn't have been nicer or more supportive. When I had to leave to attend my grandfather's funeral in the last week of November, I was supposed to film a scene that day—a wide shot of the Dread Pirate Roberts exiting his boat. But Rob told me not to worry, that I should go "because family always comes first."

"Don't sweat it, Cary," he said. "We'll use Andy Bradford to double you."

As I said, when you're on a movie set, your coworkers can become like your family.

On the 21st of November, I filmed my final scene in the film: the now famous movie-ending kiss between Westley and Buttercup. That day was a busy one, with the call sheet being peppered with a lot of pick-up shots that were needed, which we would be shooting in various stages on the Shepperton lot. Prior to the kiss scene we shot a scene that actually never ended up in the movie. It was supposed to be an alternate ending where, after Peter Falk leaves the bedroom, Fred Savage picks up *The Princess Bride* book and is looking through it, at which point he hears something outside his window. He goes to open it only to find all four of us—myself, Robin, Mandy, and André—on top of four gray stallions outside his house beckoning him to join us on our next adventure. Kind of like the concept behind *Time Bandits* where the kid's dreams come true and the fantasy becomes a reality.

It was to be shot against a black backdrop (there were no green screens in those days) and I was provided with a special Lipizzaner stallion in order to do a specific stunt. Lipizzaners are famous for doing special tricks and maneuvers, and I was supposed to get the horse to rear up on its hind legs in a heroic fashion by giving it a certain cue using the heels of my boots. I had practiced for weeks with this horse between sword-training until I got it right, and thankfully the beautiful creature did not let us down when the cameras began rolling. The horse wrangler had also provided this huge Clydesdale, the kind you see on Budweiser ads, for André, as that was the biggest they could find. And they had to build some steps for him to climb onto the animal. But this Clydesdale, as big as it was, took one look at André and refused to let him sit on his back. So the stunt team, who had prepared for this eventuality, had a standby harness built to André's specifications brought out, realizing that the only way to get him on this horse was to lower him gently in place while wired to a huge pulley, allowing him to appear to be on the horse without any weight actually touching it.

In the end Rob felt that the idea was too confusing for audiences.

ROB REINER

So we've got to do this scene where we had to have them on the four horses, and they were going to be suspended, so we shot it against black. It was going to be a visual effect. Well, André weighed like 500 pounds, so he couldn't just sit on any horse. We had to rig a system where we would lower him down with pulleys and we'd paint the cables out so he would just be resting on the horse. So we get to the end of the day and it's about eight o'clock at night, and I'm walking to the soundstage where we're going to shoot this. And they open the doors, and I see a 500-pound giant being lowered from the ceiling and he's going, "Hello, boss!" And I'm thinking, What do I do for a living here? What is this job that I have? It was pretty crazy.

That the two worlds should not meet. And it turned out to be the better choice.

After we finished that shot, it was time for Robin and I to shoot my last scene. Since Mandy and André had to go shoot other scenes with the second unit involving the tavern, I said my good-byes to them after we finished, hugging them both. I believe I became a little misty-eyed when I tried to wrap my arms around André. I couldn't believe that our journey was coming to an end.

Robin and I were then led over to another part of the soundstage where we were to sit on our horses against a beautiful sunset backdrop and perform the magical kiss. This would be my actual last scene in the film and it couldn't have been a more appropriate way to end the movie for me. Once again a crowd had gathered to witness the moment. Watching and smiling, maybe dabbing away a tear or two. This last embrace shared by Buttercup and Westley is described thusly by the Grandfather in his narration:

Since the invention of the kiss . . . there have been five kisses that have been rated the most passionate, the most pure. This one left them all behind.

We certainly did our best, Robin and I, to live up to that lofty standard. And, even though Rob would often shoot multiple takes on any given scene until he felt comfortable that he got exactly what he wanted, when it came to this particular kissing scene, Robin and I kept asking for more takes. I think we were actually so giddy we were giggling like a couple of schoolkids.

After the first take, Rob called out, "Cut and print!"

"Ummm, I'm sorry, I didn't quite feel right about that one, Rob. Can we try again?" I asked sheepishly, stifling a laugh.

Rob just smiled and said, "Sure, Cary. Why not?"

After the second take, again Rob said, "Print that!"

Then Robin asked for another.

"Yeah! We need to go again, Rob, please."

Then I asked for another.

So it went, three more takes, all of which concluded with the same directive from Rob: "Cut and print!"

We ended up shooting six takes of that kiss. After printing them all, Rob finally turned to Ceri, our script supervisor, and said after the last one, "That's a beauty! Print that, too." He then walked up to us on our horses and said:

"Uh, guys? I think we got it!"

Giggles aside, and I can't speak for Robin, but I could have gone on shooting that scene all day, as I don't think I wanted the movie to end. It was also a very tender way to end the movie. Sealing it with a kiss, so to speak.

There was a brief silence followed by an overwhelming applause as Rob announced, "Ladies and gentlemen . . . That's a wrap on Cary Elwes!"

I remember being very moved by this moment and trying hard to control my emotions as I gave a small speech thanking everyone on the crew and my fellow cast members. I turned to Robin and told her that no one could have personified the inner and outer beauty of Buttercup more wonderfully than she had. And finally, with a frog of unusual size in my throat, I turned to Rob and thanked him for being so incredibly amazing to work with and for making the experience such a joyful one not just for me but for everyone involved, which was followed by the longest bear hug I ever received from him. I ended by saying what was on my mind and perhaps the minds of many, that I wish we could go on shooting the film forever but that, sadly, all good things eventually have to come to an end.

After I was done there were lots of hugs and tears as I said my good-byes to everyone present. Robin came over and hugged me one last time. Of all the people on the film, I think I had bonded with her the most, as nearly all of our scenes in the movie had been just the two of us. I will always love her, and we will always remain close, because what we shared was a unique bond: for that brief, shining moment in time, we *were* Westley and Buttercup. A fairy-tale love that will forever be immortalized on the screen.

ROBIN WRIGHT

It was so beautiful, the story, the true love for Westley, the true love for Buttercup . . . Cary was so perfect in that role. He was so dashing and funny and good-looking and debonair. I think we'll always have a special relationship because of this film.

After the movie ended, everyone went their separate ways. I don't even recall if there was a wrap party. I'm sure there was, but I was spending a lot of time with my family, given the loss of my grandfather, and so might have missed it. Or I might simply have been too distracted by grief to go.

I didn't know how the movie would turn out. I didn't even know when or where I'd ever see any of these wonderful people again. I felt good about the film and the work we had done. There is no doubt that we all had

MANDY PATINKIN

The whole experience was so intense—the ten hours a day of filming, and working with gifted people. And Rob's gentility and his generosity as a director. And his love of actors. And all of us kids, like Cary and Robin and me, being in this joyous, gifted piece by Bill Goldman. Now we were moving on, and who knew what it would be? Whether anyone would see it or not?

CHRIS GUEST

The thing about movies is no one knows if they've done something special. I think what you do know is you've had a fantastic time. From Rob's standpoint, there was no way he was going to know before cutting it together what the film really was. You know you have great stuff but you don't really know. People have asked me about *Spinal Tap:* "Did you know?" It would be preposterous and arrogant to say we knew this was going to be something. It was just having fun with your friends. You're laughing, you're doing a thing, and that's basically it. And then you go on to some other thing.

ROBIN WRIGHT

While making a movie, you never imagine or project, assume or presume, whether the movie is going to work, or whether people will respond to it. I just know that I loved going in to work everyday and making what we were making together on *The Princess Bride*. In your mind's eye, you see the pieces fit together into a story of cohesion, and you think, whoa, this is great. We're experiencing this. But you never know if it's going to translate. Well, this one did. We had the greatest time together and I never laughed so hard in my life.

boundless faith in Rob's ability to create something special. But we didn't really know how it would be received. As an actor, you never know. You finish one job and, if you are as fortunate as I have been in my career, you are on to the next. Maybe *The Princess Bride* would come and go. Maybe it would be just another line on the résumé. Of course, we were all praying it wouldn't be.

Only time would tell.

✤ 13 ✤

A FAIRY-TALE ENDING

he Princess Bride had been originally scheduled for a big summer
release. The film's distributor, 20th Century Fox, was enthusiastic
about the movie's chances and slated it to open on July 31, 1987.
But since Rob was still editing at that time, the date was postponed. I
do recall a few months later being invited to view a rough cut of the
film on the Fox lot with my then agent, Ed Limato (who has, sadly,
since passed away). I remember being particularly nervous at the time,
as some of the giants in the comedy world—Mel Brooks, Gene Wilder,
Gilda Radner, and Carl Reiner—were going to be in attendance along
with the rest of Rob's family and close friends.

It's a strange thing, seeing a film again after such a length of time
has passed, in part because you've moved on to other projects, but also it
seems like eons ago when you made it. It's almost like a dream that has
begun to fade slowly from one's memory. However, watching the film

even in its rough form, with all the temp music and cue lines running through the picture, I thought it was a joyous, heartwarming, funny, sweet, and sincerely memorable movie. But perhaps I was just biased. I do know that the audience appeared to love it, too. But maybe, being Rob's friends and family, they were biased as well. After the screening, I remember feeling overwhelmed as I received perhaps some of the greatest and most treasured compliments of my career when Mel, Gene, Gilda, and Carl each took turns congratulating me on my performance.

When *The Hollywood Reporter* suggested in an article on September 15 that the movie would be "a challenge for the marketing department," the studio decided to push the release date even further back, opening with a limited run (meaning fewer theaters) in New York and Los Angeles on September 25, to see how it fared before going wide (meaning more theaters) a few weeks later.

The first time I saw the final version was at what was then known as Toronto's Festival of Festivals (now the Toronto International Film Festival) on September 18, a week before the official release date in the States.

Even after all this time we still didn't know what to expect. As Bill Goldman says about our industry in his fascinating book *Adventures in the Screen Trade*, "Nobody knows anything!" For if they did, he correctly reasons, everybody would be making hit movies all the time. Nobody sets out to make a bad movie. You work hard, put your faith in the material and the director, and then . . . well, you hope for the best. Truthfully, there is so much that can go wrong that it's advisable not to dwell on it, which is also Goldman's advice. If it had been up to the audience at the festival, we would've been a smash hit. They loved it. They laughed in all the right places and appeared to be moved in all the right places as well.

After the credits rolled and the lights came up, the audience stood and cheered. It was truly overwhelming. I remember looking over at Rob.

He was beaming. The audience really took the film to heart and voted it as the winner of the People's Choice Award at the festival. It seemed like the movie had a real shot.

Then came the heartache.

As we were flying back to LA, Rob unfurled a copy of what the studio had chosen for the movie poster, and we were all pretty shocked.

Apparently *The Hollywood Reporter* had been correct in their assumption. The studio's marketing department had been at a complete loss as to how they should sell the film. The poster had no image of the title character, Buttercup. No Westley. No Miracle Max. No Inigo. No Fezzik. No swordfight. Not even an R.O.U.S. in sight! Instead they opted for a one-sheet depicting a silhouette of Fred Savage and Peter Falk sitting together against a Maxfield Parrish–type background. Very sweet, but it seemed to be an odd, static choice for a movie that promised so much more. Clearly they were scrambling at the time, trying to figure out what type of movie to promote. And for some reason they decided to push the story of the Grandfather and the Grandson—in essence, a kid's movie. Granted, that relationship was an integral part of the story, but we all felt, including Rob, that perhaps it wasn't the best angle to promote the movie. And we were right, as it obviously left audiences confused and some potential filmgoers deterred.

To give you a sense of how clueless even the foreign marketing folks were, I remember someone showing me an Italian one-sheet that, granted, had an R.O.U.S. and Buttercup, but it also bizarrely featured a hawk and had Inigo as an Arnold Schwarzenegger lookalike from *Conan the Barbarian* holding his giant Barbarian sword up to his face in that iconic pose. I guess the theory was that if Arnold could sell tickets, why not give it a shot. Compounding this was the fact that, domestically, Fox had opted out of publicizing the movie at all in the media. We had no

CHRIS SARANDON
The movie poster didn't really tell you anything about the movie. The subsequent posters did feature characters from the movie, and gave you a real sense of what the movie was about. But originally it was like, What do we got here, folks? We don't know, so let's just throw it out there and see what happens. I was very disappointed when the movie was first released because I just thought, This is really a very special piece of work, and it's not going to be the sort of thing that everybody gets; it may take some time. And that has proven to be the case.

paid ads on TV or even a trailer in the theater. Indeed, the first and only trailer was considered so confusing, it was subsequently pulled from the cinemas by the studio. It all seemed like a recipe for disaster. And yet . . . despite all this the reviews, upon opening, were generally positive. A sampling:

- *The Philadelphia Inquirer:* "Given that Reiner's first feature was the riotously parodic *This Is Spinal Tap,* there is a built-in expectation here that he satirize swashbuckler derring-do. But what's captivating about *Bride* is the sincerity with which Reiner tells his story, which is sweet like cider and (fortunately) not like honey."
- *The New York Times:* "*The Princess Bride* has sweetness and sincerity on its side, and when it comes to fairy tales, those are major assets. It also has a delightful cast and a cheery, earnest style that turns out to be even more disarming as the film moves along. Even the little boy, who's a tough customer, is eventually won over."
- *Chicago Sun-Times* (Roger Ebert): "*The Princess Bride* reveals itself as a sly parody of sword and sorcery movies, a film

that somehow manages to exist on two levels at once. While younger viewers will sit spellbound at the thrilling events on the screen, adults, I think, will be laughing a lot."

Some critics, though, were reluctant to give the film anything more than a backhanded compliment, with the attitude, "Hey, it's a cute movie, and if you need something to do in the afternoon, go ahead and take your kids."

Others were simply put off by the apparent meshing of genres.

One critic, for example, had this to say: "This is a post-modern fairy tale that challenges and affirms the conventions of a genre that may not be flexible enough to support such horseplay."

Hmm. Really? I think Mr. Goldman put it best when he wrote, "Cynics are simply thwarted romantics."

Two weeks after the Toronto festival, and after the initial wave of mostly positive reviews, we all gathered once again for a screening at the New York Film Festival at the Ziegfeld Theater on 54th Street. Rob went onstage and introduced the film, then invited us all afterward to join him up there so he could introduce us. Later that night, we all gathered for dinner, where Rob got up and gave a speech:

"I just want you all to know that whatever happens with this movie, I am very proud of the work we did. But more importantly of all the hard work you did to help make this one of the most memorable experiences of my career. It's a very special film. And one, I think, we can all be proud of."

Everyone applauded. There was a general feeling in the room of camaraderie where we felt that we had made something special.

Sadly, Rob's comments about the success of the film turned out to be somewhat prophetic. The numbers were not what we had hoped for. Nor what the studio had hoped for, for that matter. After the opening

MANDY PATINKIN

I saw a rough cut of the film very early on, before it was released. And I remember I was weeping when it was over. My wife was sitting next to me and she said, "What's the matter?" And I looked at her and I said, "I never dreamed that I'd be in anything like this. I can't believe this happened before I even had time to dream it." And I couldn't get over it. That was such a high. Then I remember feeling sad when it wasn't received well. I heard that the studio didn't know how to market it—as an adventure story or a children's story . . . who knew? And so it just sort of came and went.

FRED SAVAGE

They didn't know how to market it. Didn't know what it was. Is it an adventure? Is it romantic? Is it funny? Is it moving? Is it thrilling? Is it a children's story? Is it an adult's story? And the answer is . . . yes! I think any audience can find something in the film that speaks to them, because it does have its toes in so many styles, genres, and tones. It means something to everyone, no matter what you want from the movie.

ROB REINER

Looking back, I was really stupid. I remember talking to Barry Diller, the head of Fox at the time, and I remembered that when *The Wizard of Oz* came out, it wasn't well received. People didn't understand it. They didn't like it, even though it has since become this great, enduring classic over the years. And I said to Barry, "This is terrible. We've got a movie that everybody loves but we can't get anybody to come. I don't want this to become *The Wizard of Oz!*" And he said, "Rob, don't let anybody ever hear you say that." And he was right, you know? We should be so lucky to get *The Wizard of Oz*.

weekend, we could already tell that the movie wasn't going to be a huge box office draw, something that confounded us all. Looking back I only wish the Internet had existed in 1987. I suspect that social media would have raised awareness of the film's unique quality and helped propel it to blockbuster status. Alas, movies in those days relied on traditional platforms for publicity and we didn't even have that going for us.

After dinner, when everyone was about to go their separate ways, André asked if I wanted to go out for a nightcap. Why not? I thought. Who knew when we would get to see each other again, and I always enjoyed his company.

So I joined him as he squeezed into the large chauffeured van he had and set off in search of . . . well, when you're with André, you know it's always going to be an adventure.

ROB REINER

I was really happy with what we had done because we achieved exactly what we set out to do. And I was also happy with the reaction. I mean, we had test screenings that were, like the cliché, "through the roof." With something like 94 percent of viewers saying they would definitely recommend the movie. The thing that was frustrating for me is that Fox, who was releasing the film domestically, didn't know how to market it. They had no idea what to do with it. They couldn't cut a suitable trailer. They couldn't get a one-sheet newspaper ad. So it was really frustrating.

ANDY SCHEINMAN

The movie wasn't as successful from a commercial standpoint as it should have been. I think it's a very soft title, especially if you don't know what it's about. And nobody knew. We couldn't get three college kids in the whole country to see this movie when it first came out. College kids would say, "Well, it sounds like it's for little kids." Even little boys would go, "It's girly and princesses and brides and all that stuff." And then when we screened it at UCLA, the audience went crazy. Because, of course, the reality is that the movie is one of the more satirical and adult-sensibility films that kids happen to like, too.

"I'll take you to some of my old haunts," he said, issuing some directions to the driver.

We drove only a short distance before pulling up in front of the first bar, a perennial favorite of André's: P. J. Clarke's on Third Avenue. And, of course, the moment we walked in, the place fell silent. Every head in the room turned to watch as André bent low as he entered through the door.

"It's really not possible for you to make a subtle entrance, is it?" I asked.

He smiled and replied, "Not always. But it's okay. They know me here."

As we sat down at the bar, the bartender immediately wandered over.

"Hey, André. Good to see you again. The usual?"

"Yes, please, Frank. And this is my friend, Cary. We just made a movie together and I wanna buy him a drink."

"Nice to meet you," I said, shaking hands with Frank.

"Any friend of André's is a friend of ours. What'll you have?"

"Just a beer please," I responded thinking I had better pace myself.

André's "usual" turned out to be his drink of choice, "the American," which he had let me try on location in Derbyshire—a combination of many hard spirits. In hindsight I'm glad I didn't try a sample of it before getting on his ATV, as I probably would have ended up with a lot worse than a broken toe. The beverage came, as expected, in a forty-ounce pitcher, the contents of which disappeared in a single gulp. And then came another. And they kept coming while I gingerly sipped my beer. We talked about work and movies, about his farm in North Carolina where he raised horses, his relatives back in France and, of course, about life. André was a man unlike any other—truly one of a kind. I remember him saying something quite poignant to me, that he would give anything to be able to spend just one day being regular size so he could go unnoticed.

"But you know what, boss?" he continued.

"What?" I asked.

"I am still grateful for my life."

"How come?" I responded.

"Because I have had an incredible one!" he said with gusto.

And he was right about that!

While we were talking, I noticed a man at the bar who seemed never to take his eyes off André. I didn't think this unusual, since André drew stares and fans wherever he went. Perhaps this guy was a serious fan. Then André gave me a nudge, an indication that it was time to move on. I remember him refusing to let me pay for the drinks. Something André would never let you do.

"No, no, boss. I got this . . . ," he said while leaving Frank a hundred-dollar tip.

We went out to the car, drove a few blocks, and wandered into another of André's haunts. There was another beer, more Americans, more conversation, more laughs.

That's the way it went, barhopping to André's haunts all over Manhattan for many hours. Thankfully, I realized very early on in the proceedings that I would be in way over my head, which is why I only ordered beer, while André inhaled his Americans three or four at a time in some cases. At one of the establishments I noticed the very same guy from the bar earlier on, sitting at a table, still staring at André. I continued to think nothing of it until we got to the next bar, and there he was again—the same guy! I leaned over to André.

"Hey, André. I think that guy is following us," I whispered conspiratorially.

"Where?" he responded, his large brow suddenly furrowing as he turned his head to look in the direction I had been looking.

I thought to myself, If this fellow turned out to be a threat, he wasn't going to remain one for long.

"Over there . . ."

I nodded in the direction of the stalker at the table, who chose to look away at that moment.

André leaned back and looked at the guy. He then turned back and nodded nonchalantly.

"Oh, don't worry about him."

"Why? Do you know the guy?"

"It's a long story."

That was enough to pique my interest.

André downed what appeared to be the last eight ounces of one of his Americans and put the jug back down on the bar. After wiping his mouth, he said, "He's a cop."

"A what?" I responded, clearly confused.

"A policeman," he replied.

It turns out that on one of his nights out barhopping, André had had a bit too much to drink. And while he was waiting for his car from the valet, he slipped and fell over. But he didn't just fall on his butt, he fell right on top of a very surprised patron. I can only imagine what that felt like for the poor unsuspecting fellow, who must have thought a building had landed on him. It could have turned out to be a major lawsuit, but I think the whole thing was settled fairly quickly and quietly. After that, the NYPD decided that whenever André went out for a drink, they would send one of their finest to follow him and make sure he didn't fall on anyone again.

"They said it was for my own safety!" This last comment brought a wry grin from André.

I certainly didn't dispute the story because, although André was very tall, he wasn't prone to telling tall tales. Anything was possible. Once he recognized the undercover cop, he bought the guy a drink at every bar from then on. The cop responded each time by holding up his glass in acknowledgment and continued to tail us for the entire night. Pretty nice gig if you can get it.

Sadly, André passed away in January of 1993 from congestive heart failure. I was shooting a Mel Brooks comedy at the time and remember being heartbroken upon learning the news. It was very hard to be funny that day. Compounding the tragedy was finding out that he was only forty-six when he died. André knew he wasn't going to live to a ripe old age and even told Billy Crystal at one point during the shoot, "We don't get such a good break, the little guys and the big guys. We don't live so long."

I think that is why André carried himself in life with that beatific smile of his. He never took a single day for granted, not knowing if it might be his last. He wanted to share how beautiful life was with everyone he came into contact with. He was as generous-hearted and sweet a person as I ever hope to meet. The kind of guy who would give you the shirt off his back, a shirt big enough for four or five people. He never let anyone pay for a meal or a drink as he wanted to be the one to give instead of receiving. This massive icon of a man taught me a lot about appreciating the small things in life and about living in the moment, and I am more than grateful to have known him . . . I feel honored. And in that vein I am grateful that at least he enjoyed the experience of making the film as much as the rest of us did. I found out from his family and friends that it had been one of the highlights of his life. They told me that after it came out, whatever city he was wrestling in (which was limited to mostly making appearances since his back operation had not been a success) he would sneak into the back of a theater where it was playing, and watch as much as he could without drawing too much attention, and told everyone he just loved it.

That memorable evening I spent with André would be one of my last adventures in making *The Princess Bride*. What was kind of sad was that it seemed destined back then to be a relatively small movie, seen by only a smattering of people. Or so we all thought.

Then, out of the blue (I guess if I had to figure out a date, it might have been around Christmas 1988), the movie started to take on a life of its own. It was a booming time for the VHS market and videos had become an enormously popular Christmas gift. And what better movie to share at Christmas than *The Princess Bride*? That first year, copies flew off the shelves—and they've been flying ever since, in one form or another.

My awareness of this phenomenon began in the strangest way, almost subtly, with the occasional fan coming up to me in public, telling me they had recently rented or bought the movie, and how much it meant to them. Within a year or so, it became commonplace. Waitresses taking my order would invariably engage in a conversation that went something along these lines:

"And how would you like that cooked?"

"Medium-rare, please."

"As you wish!" Smile. Occasional wink.

At first I didn't know how to respond. I had little practice in being in the surreal position of becoming a matinee idol, which is what Westley had suddenly become to millions of young women. It came out of nowhere. And at the time there didn't seem to be a reason for this. *The Princess Bride* had disappeared. The movie was "mostly dead," if not buried. And then, suddenly, it was everywhere. It had come back to life in a gloriously, wonderfully, and deliciously unexpected way.

The resurgence came as a complete shock to me, as I think it was for the whole cast. But bewilderment quickly gave way to gratitude. A deep, profound appreciation for the good fortune that had come my way. There's simply no other way to put it: I felt blessed. The resurgence helped to boost my film career and provide me with a truly wonderful life. Once you are recognized from a particular role or film, everything begins to change. And when the movie is as beloved as *The Princess Bride*, you have bestowed upon you something akin to immortality.

BILLY CRYSTAL

It's been one of the little jewels of my career. Very often, still to this day, in airports or movie theaters, people will walk by and go, "Have fun storming the castle!" Or the really cool ones will whisper to me, "Don't go swimming for an hour, a good hour," and then just walk away. Those are the really cool ones.

Among the acknowledged fans of *The Princess Bride* are people who have held some of the most prominent and influential positions in the world. On June 1, 1988, I got a chance to visit the Vatican with my mother. Through a series of contacts and connections she arranged a brief audience with His then Holiness Pope John Paul II. I didn't realize at the time that the pope had a great love of the arts. Moreover, I wouldn't learn until later when I played him in a TV movie that as a young man in Poland he had been an actor, a poet, and a playwright. He was incredibly literate and well read. In essence, a true Renaissance man. But who would have guessed that his interests extended deep into popular culture as well?

So imagine my surprise when we posed together for a photo, and the pope turned to me and smiled upon recognizing me.

"Ah . . . You are the actor!"

"Yes, Your Holiness."

"The one from *The Princess and the Bride!*" he said, miscalculating the title in a very sweet way that many people still do.

I was stunned.

"Your Holiness . . . ," I stammered. "You've . . . you've seen the movie?"

He nodded approvingly.

"Yes, yes. Very good film. Very funny."

As I write this, Pope John Paul II has just been canonized at the Vatican, which I guess means we can literally count a saint among the admirers of our film. Who knew?

Some years later, on March 5, 1998, I discovered that the film had fans high up in the government as well. I had recently finished filming a few episodes of an HBO miniseries produced by Tom Hanks entitled *From the Earth to the Moon.* The series, about NASA's Apollo program, in which I portrayed Michael Collins from Apollo 11, hadn't yet aired, but luckily for us, it was given a rather spectacular and unprecedented liftoff. One day I got an unexpected call from Tom himself.

"Please hold for Mr. Hanks," his assistant said on the phone.

Then Tom came on the line.

"Hey, Cary," he said, jovially. "What are you doing two weeks from Saturday?" he said, getting straight to the point.

"Not a lot, why?"

"Well, how do you feel about going to the White House?" he asked in that wonderful playful way only Tom Hanks can.

"That's a pretty silly question," I jokingly responded. "What's the event?"

He explained that it just so happened that the Clintons were big fans of the NASA space program, and they wanted to screen one of our episodes, specifically mine dealing with Apollo 11, as part of the White House's Millennium Series.

"So get yourself a nice suit, and we'll see you in a couple of weeks, okay?" he said before signing off.

Since the series had twelve episodes, I was indeed fortunate that the one the Clintons chose happened to be the one I was in.

So my then fiancée (now my wife) and I flew to Washington, as part of an entourage that included of course Tom Hanks and his wonderfully talented wife, Rita, fellow producers Ron Howard and Brian Grazer, then HBO chairman Jeff Bewkes, and head of HBO programming Chris Albrecht. All the available Apollo astronauts were invited, which was very cool, along with myself and my cast mates, Bryan Cranston and Tony Goldwyn. It was an amazing evening, during which President Clinton revealed in a speech that Hillary, as a young girl, had once written a letter to NASA expressing an interest in becoming an astronaut—a comment that brought big laughs from the audience. The late John F. Kennedy Jr. was also there with his beautiful fiancée, Carolyn Bessette, and delivered a very moving speech in which he declared the space program to be his father's "proudest legacy."

After the screening there was a big reception in one of the rooms in the West Wing. The place was packed, and in the center of the room, in the middle of this incredible swarm of activity, was the tallest man in the place: President Clinton himself. I remember thinking of it in movie terms—that if you had filmed this scene from above, it would have resembled a whirlpool-like vortex of people, all hoping to get closer to the epicenter where the president stood. All hoping, like ourselves, for a two-minute audience with the most powerful, and maybe the most charismatic, man on the planet. And yet, as strange as this informal meet-and-greet seemed, it all sort of worked.

My fiancée and I patiently waited in line, and eventually we found ourselves standing in front of the president. I stuck out my hand and began to speak.

"Mr. President, my name is . . ."

I got no further than that, when he interrupted me with that wonderful Arkansas accent of his.

"I know exactly who you are, Cary," he said warmly, like we were old buddies, rather than two people who had never met before. As he shook my hand, he flashed that million-dollar smile of his. It was like staring into a set of blinding headlights.

Instantly I wondered whether something had turned up in my background check, the one performed on virtually all White House guests before they can be granted access. The anxiety must have been obvious, as the president quickly put me at ease.

"Oh, no, no . . . It's not what you think," he said, still smiling broadly. "I just wanted you to know that Chelsea and I are huge fans of *The Princess Bride*."

Chelsea is, of course, Bill and Hillary's daughter. I tried to picture them together, watching the movie like any other family. It seemed at once sweet and surreal.

"You were great in this movie tonight," he added, referring to *From the Earth to the Moon*. "But you were fantastic as Westley. I just love that movie! Chelsea and I must have seen it over a hundred times. I can quote almost every line."

I was, of course, both flattered and speechless. I managed to respond, "Thank you, Mr. President. That means a great deal to me."

After introducing my fiancée, who was standing right next to me, she quickly seized the moment.

"Mr. President, what if Cary sent Chelsea an autographed copy of the script? Do you think she would like that?"

The president immediately locked eyes with her.

"You know what, Lisa Marie?" he said. "I think she'd like that a great deal."

He then turned back to me. "You think you could do that for her, Cary?"

"Absolutely, Mr. President. It would be my pleasure," I quickly responded.

As soon as we got back to the hotel, I called Rob. I couldn't wait to share the news.

"Did you know the president was a fan?" I asked.

"You're kidding."

He was just as dumbfounded and delighted as I was.

A few weeks later I sent Chelsea the signed script. And a few days after that, I received a very gracious thank-you letter from President Clinton, which still hangs on the wall of my office.

People have often asked me what my strangest encounter with a fan was. I once met a young lady who politely introduced herself, then proceeded to tell me how much the movie meant to her. After she was done she swept aside her long hair to reveal a freshly imprinted and very

ROB REINER

I have had many encounters with many people from all walks of life who love the movie. But the strangest had to be this one: One night Nora Ephron and her husband, Nick Pileggi, who wrote the screenplay to the movie *Goodfellas*, wanted to take me to a restaurant in New York where the mobster John Gotti liked to eat. So we went, and sure enough, in walks Gotti with six wiseguys. After we finished the meal I walk outside and there's one of these goodfellas standing in front of a huge limo who looked just like Luca Brasi from *The Godfather*. He looks down at me and he goes, "Hey! You killed my father. Prepare to die!" And I just froze. Then he starts laughing and says: "*The Princess Bride*! I love that movie!" I almost fell over right in the street!

red tattoo of the words *As you wish* in ornate calligraphy on the back of her neck. She asked me to sign it with a Sharpie so she could add my signature as a tattoo. Naturally I hesitated, wondering whether it was appropriate or not, but her mother, who was standing right next to her, insisted.

It's humbling, to say the least, to realize that you are part of something that has touched a lot of people's hearts (and skin). As I've said many times, I'm sure that my tombstone will probably bear the words *As You Wish*, and I'm totally cool with that. It's a wonderful thing to be associated with such a beautiful, funny, warmhearted movie. One whose popularity has shown no sign of waning.

A quarter century later, the entire cast (minus those who have sadly passed on—André, Peter Falk, Peter Cook, and Mel Smith) assembled, not merely as an act of nostalgia, but to celebrate something that has remained as vibrant today as it was when it was first released.

That much was evident when we got together at Lincoln Center, as the crowd cheered with the entrance of each character on-screen, and shouted along with famous lines, working themselves up into a fervor. It was wonderful to experience that kind of response with the people who made it happen, some of whom I hadn't seen in years.

Watching the movie again twenty-five years later I am in awe of how

MANDY PATINKIN

It was one of the true privileges of my life to be asked to have been in this film. And most of all, to get to have lived long enough to witness what it has become, to see the pleasure it has brought to so many generations. I had no idea that it would have this effect on people. I guess the real pleasure of it is that this movie became far more than any of us ever dreamed or imagined.

BILLY CRYSTAL

Pretty much everybody was there at the twenty-fifth reunion at Lincoln Center. It was fantastic to see them, and there were, I don't know, maybe fifteen hundred people in the theater. I hadn't seen it with an audience since the premiere, and that was so many years ago. And back then it wasn't a big deal. But now! This was like *The Rocky Horror Picture Show*. People went berserk. It was so moving to me. When someone would make their entrance in the movie, the audience would applaud. It was like seeing a favorite actor in a Broadway show. There were noticeable tears when Peter Falk came in to read in the beginning. They chanted lines: "Inconceivable!" Applause. The Southeast Asia line. Applause. "Have fun storming the castle!" And so on. They knew all the lines. It was absolutely insane!

masterfully Rob directed it. I still stick to the theory that he was really the only director who could have pulled it off. He had the right sensibility, the right sense of humor—just the right touch to do it. The way he directed—the performances, the shots, the editing, the production value, the score, everything. There's not a single frame on-screen that wasn't supposed to be there.

After the screening we were all patting him on the back, telling him how great it still was, and all he could say was, "It's kind of fun, right?" And we were saying, "Rob! It's a great movie!" His response to that was, "You think?" He is truly filled with humility about his own gifts as a director. It is just one among many very endearing qualities he possesses.

We also found out that night that Goldman hadn't seen the movie with an audience since the initial Toronto premiere back in 1987. But he sat right behind me at the Lincoln Center event and I could hear him, because he has a very distinct voice. Every time the audience oohed, aahed, cheered, laughed, or recited a line, Bill would practically gush:

"Oh, my goodness. This is incredible!" He was stunned by the reception. And afterward, as we prepared to go onstage and answer questions in front of a live audience, I found myself standing next to him.

"Well, Bill, what do ya think?" I asked.

"I had no idea," he said incredulously. "It's incredible. They knew every line. They loved it!"

I smiled and gave him a hug. "Of course they did, Bill. You wrote something beautiful."

Bill nodded. For a moment it looked as though he might start weeping with joy. But before he could do that, Rob took the stage and the crowd roared. After he thanked the audience for coming, he began calling us out onto the stage and we all took our seats next to one another

WILLIAM GOLDMAN

This movie was a remarkable experience—the best experience I've ever had. It just worked. You never know why, and you wish it would work like that all the time, but it doesn't. You never know what's gonna happen with a movie when it comes out. Even if you've got a great cast and it's wonderfully directed, you just never know. All I know is it's different. It's an odd piece. But now it's become this whole thing, and I had no idea it would happen. I'll meet somebody and they'll say, "My daughter is twenty-eight and it's her favorite movie," or whatever. People seem to love it.

for a post-screening Q&A, which was moderated by the Film Society of Lincoln Center's Scott Foundas, who also organized the event. We recounted tales of making the movie. What impact the film has had on us all. All the times we have had our lines spoken back to us, etc. Wally said that he believes that everyone he meets thinks that they are the first ones to come up with the idea of saying his lines back to him. Billy told of how he recently sat down to watch the film with his two grown daughters and his grandchildren, which was the "as you wish" moment for him, and how love for the film will most likely endure through generations.

Then Bill, who was still very emotional from the screening, was asked a very poignant question about whether or not there was any chance he would finish the sequel, entitled *Buttercup's Baby*, a chapter of which is included in the thirtieth-anniversary edition of the novel. Bill sort of broke down a little bit, saying, "I've been trying for twenty years to do it. I'm desperate to write it but I don't know how . . . I would love to make it happen, more than anything else I've not written, but I can't . . . I can't crack the story." It was very moving.

At one point a young man from the audience asked Robin if she would take a "selfie" with him, as it would fulfill a boyhood dream of his. Robin of course graciously complied. I was then asked to do my impersonation of Fat Albert that so impressed Rob on our first meeting and of course I couldn't let the audience down. The evening was one of the most enjoyable experiences of my career. I only hope that we get to do it again in five more years . . . or even ten. Perhaps a golden anniversary of *The Princess Bride*?

Inconceivable? Maybe not.

Why has this film endured when so many others haven't? What is it about this particular film that struck a nerve with audiences around the world to make it the beloved movie it is today? And I'm not suggesting it is *Citizen Kane*, but it has endured. There are many theories, but truthfully I don't think anyone really knows. Does anyone know anything about what makes a good movie? Mr. Goldman, we know, thinks not. I have a theory. So for what it's worth, here it is . . . I think that the film has endured because it was made with a lot of heart. And for that we really have to look at the creative and tender hearts of Bill Goldman and Rob Reiner. Both men are very different people who came from very different backgrounds, but they share one thing in common . . . they have

FRED SAVAGE

I remember years ago, I think I was in high school, or just in college, I ran into Mandy. Just completely randomly, walking past him on the street. We had never met, since we didn't share one minute of screen time. And we had nothing in common other than this movie. And I was like, "I think we have to hug, right? We're both part of this thing." And we did! We hugged! And I felt this real connection with him, because this thing just pulled all these people together. I feel like my experience was unique in that I wasn't part of the camaraderie of the filmmaking. It was very separate, in the film and in the shooting. And so I never met most of these people. But we still have this common experience that's kind of forever linked us all.

CAROL KANE

It's almost like a real family. You know, when you all get to sit down together. And now, because this movie is lasting, it continues to happen. Which really is another privilege.

BILLY CRYSTAL

It's like a great old hat that you can pass down that somebody of the next generation can wear and it still fits, you know? That's what it is. Also, you can sit there with a little one next to you and you don't have to worry about putting your hands over his eyes because there's something scary or over their ears because they shouldn't hear something. Everything's done with a charm. The Rodents of Unusual Size, the Shrieking Eels—it's all done in a playful kind of way. If you look at those rodents, you know there's a little person inside. I mean, you just know, but I think that's what it's about.

never lost touch with the love in their hearts for storytelling. And in this film they were able to explore that love of storytelling in a way they perhaps will never be able to again: the telling of the most extraordinary fairy tale/adventure story about storytelling that can now be counted as a classic.

The film is indeed magical. It makes you feel many different things upon every viewing. As Billy Crystal has said, it makes you feel good. It makes you miss your childhood. It makes you want to have someone read stories to you again. It makes you want to kiss your sweetheart, fight a duel, or ride a white horse into the sunset . . . all in the name of love. In short, it's the perfect fairy tale.

As I look through my pile of fan mail I know that even today this film continues to touch the hearts of so many children, teenagers, and adults around the world. We grow old but it doesn't seem to. It has discovered the fountain of youth. It is still out there, expanding and growing in ways we could never have imagined, and in ways we can't control. We don't own it anymore. None of us do—not I, nor any of the other cast members. Not Rob Reiner, not Norman Lear. Maybe not even Bill Goldman.

It belongs to everyone now.

And if you are among those who enjoyed this film half as much as we did making it, then all I can say is . . .

Well . . . you know.

EPILOGUE

I was working on a deadline to finish my own memoir when I was invited to attend the twenty-fifth-anniversary screening of Rob Reiner's film of William Goldman's glorious, one-of-a-kind book *The Princess Bride*, starring the author of the volume for which I delightedly write this epilogue, Cary Elwes.

While I couldn't get to New York and Lincoln Center, where an audience of over a thousand fans ecstatically shouted out one memorable line after another along with the actors on the screen, at least a dozen people phoned and texted me as to the enormous success of the screening.

Nothing I have ever been connected to has had a greater and more loving impact on its audience. Let me be quick to say I had nothing to do with *The Princess Bride* creatively. My erstwhile associate Mark E. Pollack oversaw the filming from a business standpoint; I simply fell in love with Goldman's book, then his screenplay, and agreed to finance the film. It stunned me that every studio had turned it down, even with the likes of Norman Jewison, Robert Redford, and François Truffaut attached to it. Having worked with Rob Reiner for nine years I knew it was right up Rob's alley—which is where I lived as well. William Goldman's script was deliciously faithful to his book and Rob Reiner bringing Bill's characters to life was the perfect prescription for a heart-warming and hilarious film.

Rob and his partner, Andy Scheinman, cast the picture brilliantly, what with Robin Wright as Buttercup; Mandy Patinkin as Inigo Montoya; Wallace Shawn as Vizzini; Billy Crystal as Miracle Max; André the Giant as Fezzik; Peter Falk as the Grandfather; Chris Sarandon as Prince Humperdinck; Carol Kane as Valerie; Fred Savage as the Grandson; Peter Cook as the Impressive Clergyman; and, of course, Cary Elwes, the only actor I could ever imagine as Westley.

The Princess Bride has to be one of the most beloved—not a word used often in this context—pieces of cinema extant. Nothing has made me more proud than my relationship to it.

—Norman Lear

ACKNOWLEDGMENTS

You've heard the saying "it takes a village to raise a child." Well, it takes a small village to write a book. I have to start by acknowledging Joe Layden, who co-wrote the book with me. I couldn't have done it without him, and I am forever indebted to the amount of work he put in to the process. I must also thank William Goldman, whose approval I needed to write the book in the first place. Since *The Princess Bride* is still his favorite material, he was naturally unsure about the idea at first. But after a few conversations on the phone, during which I explained how it would be tenderly approached, he finally relented and gave me permission. And for that I am truly grateful; otherwise I would not be sitting here writing any of this. I am also grateful for his books *Adventures in the Screen Trade* and *Which Lie Did I Tell?*, which were a joy to reread after so many years and gave me a fascinating insight into his state of mind during the process of trying to get the film off the ground in the first place.

Next is our superlative producer, Norman Lear, who I thank not only for his wonderful epilogue, but for providing me with all the call sheets and script notes, which he said would help jog my memory. He was right, they most certainly did. I also have to thank him for sharing all the wonderful photographs from Act III's private collection, which now grace this tome. Indeed I am truly grateful to all the folks at Act III—especially Julie Dyer, Penny Wright, Jackie Jensen, and their archivist, Jean Andersen—for assisting me in the research for this book.

I have to thank Rob Reiner for his great foreword, and also thank him, Andy Scheinman, and the whole cast—including Robin Wright, Billy Crystal, Mandy Patinkin, Christopher Guest, Chris Sarandon, Carol Kane, Wallace Shawn, and Fred Savage—for contributing their memories to the book. This book might have my and Joe Layden's names on the cover as authors, but these guys all took time out of their busy schedules to share remembrances about their personal experiences on the making of the film, without which this book would not have been possible. I am also grateful to André's family, friends, and associates, who helped fill in his feelings about the film, especially to Robin Christensen and Marc Spiegel. I am also deeply indebted to my dear friend, Birgit Michelini, for making all those visits to the Vatican archives on our behalf.

I have to thank my publisher, Touchstone, for having faith in me to pull this off in the first place. Thanks go to my editor, Matthew Benjamin, who gently nurtured my writing journey, and to all the other folks at Touchstone and Simon & Schuster who helped in the creation of this book and supported me and taught me a great deal in the process, including Sophie Vershbow, Brian Belfiglio, Meredith Vilarello, David

Falk, Jessica Chin, Laura Flavin, Elaine Wilson, and last but not least, Susan Moldow and Sally Kim.

I am seriously indebted to the talented Shepard Fairey for designing the magnificent print which appears on the opening pages. And to his wife, Amanda, for helping to make it happen. It turned out greater than we could have imagined. (And if you would like to learn a little bit more about Shepard Fairey, just turn the page.) I need to thank my manager Ben Levine, who suggested the idea for this book in the first place and never wavered in his belief that it would come to pass. And I want to thank my other manager, Ryan Bundra, and my agent, Katherine Latshaw, for helping make the deal happen.

I would be remiss if I didn't give thanks to my incredibly patient wife, Lisa Marie, who had to endure my being sequestered for weeks at a time in order to make the many deadlines for this book. Being apart from my family was perhaps the hardest part of the process of writing this mini-memoir and I am grateful to her and our daughter for being so understanding (and to Skype for helping make it a little less unbearable!).

Finally, I want to thank the incredibly loyal fans of *The Princess Bride*, who now span generations. You are the ones who have continued to keep this film alive after a quarter century, and thus made this book possible. I am forever indebted to you all.

Your humble Westley,

C. E.

S hepard Fairey was born in Charleston, South Carolina. He received his Bachelor of Fine Arts in Illustration at the Rhode Island School of Design in Providence, Rhode Island. While at R.I.S.D. he created the "OBEY GIANT" art campaign, with imagery that has changed the way people see art and the urban landscape. His work has evolved into an acclaimed body of art that includes the 2008 "HOPE" portrait of Barack Obama, which can be found in the Smithsonian's National Portrait Gallery.

Since the start of his career in 1989, he has exhibited in galleries and museums around the world, both indoor with his fine art and outdoor with his street art and murals. His works are in the permanent collections of the Museum of Modern Art (MoMA), the Victoria and Albert Museum, the Boston Institute of Contemporary Art, the San Francisco Museum of Modern Art, and many others.

For more information, visit www.obeygiant.com.

INDEX

Note: Italic page numbers refer to illustrations.

ABOUT THE AUTHOR

photo credit: Lance Straedler

CARY ELWES is a British born actor, author, and screenplay writer. He starred in *The Princess Bride* before moving on to roles in *Robin Hood: Men in Tights, Glory, Days of Thunder, Twister,* and *Saw,* among many other acclaimed performances. He recently starred in Rob Reiner's new film *Being Charlie* and was also reunited with Mandy Patinkin in the soon to be released film *The Queen of Spain.* Additionally, Elwes cowrote the screenplay for *Elvis & Nixon* and is currently filming the acclaimed TV series, *The Art of More.* He lives in Los Angeles with his wife and daughter. Find out more about Cary Elwes on Twitter @Cary_Elwes.

JOE LAYDEN has authored or coauthored more than thirty books, including multiple *New York Times* bestsellers.